BusinessWeek

INNOVATION
Power Plays

D0881959

INNOVATION
Power Plays

How the World's

Hottest Change Agents

Reach the Top of Their Game

McGraw-Hill

New York · Chicago · San Francisco
Lisbon · London · Madrid · Mexico City · Milan
New Delhi · San Juan · Seoul · Singapore
Sydney · Toronto

1 2 3 4 5 6 7 8 9 0 DOC/DOC 0 9 8

ISBN-13 978-0-07-148631-6
MHID   0-07-148631-3

This publication is designed to provide accurate and authoritative information in regard to the subject matter covered. It is sold with the understanding that neither the author nor the publisher is engaged in rendering legal, accounting, or other professional service. If legal advice or other expert assistance is required, the services of a competent professional person should be sought.

—From a Declaration of Principles jointly adopted
by a Committee of the American Bar Association
and a Committee of Publishers

McGraw-Hill books are available at special quantity discounts to use as premiums and sales promotions, or for use in corporate training programs. To contact a representative please visit the Contact Us pages at www.mhprofessional.com.

This book is printed on acid-free paper.

CONTENTS

INTRODUCTION

BusinessWeek readers tell us how busy their professional lives have become and how important it is to get their business news, information, and ideas delivered in a concise and authoritative fashion. We do that each week in the magazine, and every day at BusinessWeek.com. But we also know that businesspeople need to delve deeply into areas that will help them manage more effectively. That's why we have created the Power Plays series in collaboration with McGraw-Hill Professional books. Each book draws from *BusinessWeek*'s in-depth reporting on exceptional leaders as they face strategic challenges on a variety of fronts.

The Power Plays chapters address real-life situations where best practices are at work in companies large and small. To make the narratives more useful, we have distilled information designed to help enhance your performance in today's complex business environment. This information is presented in readily digestible nuggets: "Lesson Plans" that articulate the key points of the case study, "Power Moves" that deliver tactical advice on how to manage change, and "Monday Morning" strategies that focus on achieving success and keeping progress rolling.

The Power Plays volume you are now reading is an exploration of the way energetic managers drive innovation in their organizations. It's an impressive tableau, starting with Kodak's CEO Antonio Perez. With the film business on the ropes and the company's future in doubt, Perez embraced a high-stakes strategy to reinvent the inkjet printer business. At electronics giant Best Buy, Jody Thompson and Cali Ressler are "smashing the clock," freeing up work schedules and dispensing with mandatory meetings in a bold move to reinvent the workplace. Microsoft's J Allard is an iconoclast, exhorting his colleagues to think far beyond Windows to pursue the tech world's Next Big Thing. At JPMorgan, Jamie Dimon imposed financial controls while encouraging aggressive capital investments, thus offering a disciplined lesson in strategy innovation. Norbert Reithofer's innovations in management—sharing the wealth, listening to workers, and rewarding risk—are paying off big at BMW. In Europe, at Vuitton, creativity flourishes even as CEO Bernard Arnault introduces cost-cutting innovations in the manufacturing process. Henning Kagermann, meanwhile, has stepped up the pace of change at SAP by seeding a teeming ecosystem of new products. Roger Deromedi tackled Kraft's problem by slashing nonperforming brands while backing new, truly inventive, products. And marketing guru Steve Stoute shows how even stodgy brands can be reinvigorated with a dash of pop culture.

At the close of this Power Plays book, we step back and consider some of the values at the core of innovation. "Speed Demons" surveys smart companies, such as Virgin Group and H&M, that are getting products to market in a flash to gain an edge on rivals. There's a compelling lesson in their success, namely, that to flourish in today's hypercompetitive global markets, companies need to experiment freely and be willing to accept the occasional stumble. In this section, we also explore some viewpoints: an overview of the five most common mistakes in innovation, insights on making online pay, and a look at HP's cultural revolution.

One note about these case studies: They are drawn from *BusinessWeek* reporting at the time the stories were written, and therefore are snapshots in time. Every effort has been made to provide factual updates, but some of the characters and circumstances upon which the studies are based have changed. Still, we believe that these narratives stand the test of time and remain not only illuminating but replete with valuable lessons for developing successful power plays.

★　★　★

Many people at *BusinessWeek* contributed the ideas and case studies in this book, including Spencer E. Ante, Michael Arndt, Robert Berner, Diane Brady, Peter Burrows, Michelle Conlin, Gail Edmondson, Jay Greene, Steve Hamm, Mara Der Hovanesian, Louise Lee, Tom Lowry, Carol Matlack, Stanley Reed, Andy Reinhardt, Ian Rowley, Emily Thornton, Rachel Tiplady, Hiroko Tashiro, and Joseph Weber. Frank Comes, Jamie Russell, Jessica Silver-Greenberg, and Craig Sturgis developed the series with Mary Glenn and Ed Chupak, our colleagues at sister company McGraw-Hill Professional. Commentaries were provided by Pamela Kruger. Very special thanks go to Ruth Mannino for her excellent guidance on design and editorial production.

Stephen J. Adler
Editor-in-Chief
BusinessWeek

BusinessWeek

INNOVATION
Power Plays

ANTONIO M. PEREZ: KODAK'S MOMENT OF TRUTH

POWER PLAYS

The ailing film giant, led by a refugee from Hewlett-Packard, Antonio Perez, has embarked on a risky strategy to reinvent the inkjet printer.

This story by Steve Hamm, with Louise Lee and Spencer E. Ante, appeared in February 2007.

LESSON PLAN

Recognize that the business model needs to be overhauled—not just tinkered with—when the company's core business is shrinking.

Formulate clear market goals and keep a laser focus on achieving them.

Mount an effective challenge to an industry giant by creating a high-quality product that addresses customers' needs and dissatisfaction with existing goods.

Resuscitate a declining business by creating new sidelines that have the potential to grow quickly and replace lost revenues.

1

THE HOLY GRAIL

Antonio M. Perez left the consumer inkjet printer business seven years ago after he lost out to Carly Fiorina for the top slot at Hewlett-Packard. But it had never been far from his mind. That's why, a few weeks after he joined a struggling Eastman Kodak Co. as president on April 2, 2003, he was peering into a microscope in a lab on Kodak's sprawling Rochester (New York) campus. Perez was amazed at what he saw: droplets of a new ink Kodak scientists had produced that promised to yield photo prints with vivid colors that would last a lifetime. "It was the Holy Grail of inkjet printing, and they had it here," he recalls.

Ever since then, Perez and Kodak have been working on a top-secret plan, code-named Goya, to make a big entrance into the consumer inkjet printer business. For the past year, a Kodak development team has been putting the finishing touches on printer technologies in a nondescript building across the street from HP's inkjet printer lab in suburban San Diego. On February 6 [2007], it became clear what they were up to when Perez, now Kodak's chief executive, rented the *Saturday Night Live* studio in New York to unveil a line of multipurpose machines that not only handle photographs and documents but also make copies and send faxes.

The Kodak printers are designed, first and foremost, to print high-quality photos: The ink is formulated so that prints will stay vibrant for 100 years rather than 15. Most impressive of all, replacement ink cartridges will cost half of what consumers are used to paying. The new printers will arrive in stores in March, priced at $149 to $299. Black ink cartridges will cost $9.99, color $14.99. If consumers buy Kodak's economical Photo Value Pack, which combines paper and ink, the cost per print is about 10 cents, vs. 24 cents for HP's comparable package. "It's really a revolution of thought in how to bring the price of printing down and encourage people to print more," says David Morrish, senior vice president of merchandising for Best Buy Co., which has an exclusive on the product for three months.

UPENDING THE MODEL

If Kodak pulls this off—and that's a big if, considering the forces it's up against—it could pose a huge challenge to the $50 billion printer industry. Printer companies now rely on a razor-and-blades strategy, often discounting machines and making most of their profits on replacement cartridges. "We're very proud that we're coming to market 20 years late," Perez says with a grin. "We think it will give us an opportunity to disrupt the industry's business model and address consumers' key dissatisfaction: the high cost of ink."

> **POWER MOVE**
>
> Just because a company has been the market leader for years doesn't mean that a newcomer can't elbow its way in. The key: selling a better product at a lower price.

In particular, Kodak's strategy is an assault on the profit engine of industry leader HP. Printing supplied 60 percent of HP's $6.56 billion in operating earnings last year. Yet Perez claims he has no malice toward his former employer. "I spent my life there. I respect them," he says. "I'm doing this for Kodak."

Perez predicts that the inkjet printers will become a multibillion-dollar product line. He'd better be right. Kodak has struggled for years to find a replacement for its rapidly declining photo-film business. In the fourth quarter, the company posted its first profit in two years, a reflection of cost cuts, not rising sales. If he doesn't show growth soon, investors could bail out.

SCANNING OPTION

His last, best hope is to create a multifaceted printer-and-imaging business, a smaller version of the one that generated $26.8 billion in revenues for HP last year. Consumer printers are just the latest piece of that strategy: Perez already has a fast-growing but low-margin lineup of digital cameras, docking-station printers for cameras, an online site for managing and printing pictures, and a commercial inkjet business. Perez is cooking up services such as one that lets people run shoeboxes of old prints through a store scanner, quickly organizing and enhancing the images. And all the while he's been accumulating cash by shucking such major businesses as his medical imaging unit, whose sale to Onex Healthcare Holdings Inc. for $2.5 billion was announced in January.

What's been missing so far is anything that would replace the once-huge profits that Kodak made on film. Perez insists that even while charging lower prices for ink, he can extract double-digit operating margins from consumer inkjet printing within three years. He says that Kodak cut costs by putting its print heads in the machine rather than in the replacement cartridges, which saves on materials and manufacturing. Plus, Kodak is using a lot of off-the-shelf parts.

POWER MOVE

At a time when rapidly changing technology can obliterate once-thriving businesses, companies have to be prepared to reinvent themselves. Kodak, for instance, is now repositioning itself as a multifaceted printer-and-imaging business.

But Kodak is up against a juggernaut. HP enjoys a huge advantage in shelf space at stores ranging from office supply chains to supermarkets and has done a masterful job of sharing some of its printer profits with retailers. All told, HP spends about $1 billion a year on printer research and development alone, which helps it continually find ways to improve printing speed and quality. Industry analysts expect HP to sit back and wait to see if Kodak's new machines get traction. If they do, HP could respond with selective discounting. Already, there are signs that HP is ready to defend its turf with tough tactics. "[Perez] is going into a gunfight with a knife," says Nils Madden, marketing director for HP inkjets.

The February 6 unveiling of Kodak's printers signals the end of a remarkable 3$\frac{1}{2}$-year forced march to get a potentially revolutionary product out the door. Perez built his team by matching a slew of former HP colleagues with Kodak chemists and nanotechnology experts. Perhaps never before has a challenge to a major company been launched by a rival that knew it so well.

The seeds of the project were planted in the late 1990s, when HP briefly considered acquiring Kodak. During a 15-day due-diligence process, Perez looked over Kodak's patent portfolio. Although HP's board nixed the merger, Perez's prowling later resulted in a joint venture, established in 2000, to produce high-quality inkjet photo printers for retail outlets.

The project, Phogenix Imaging, was ultimately a bust, a victim of conflicts between its owners. On May 14, 2003, with the first machines ready for shipment on the loading dock and only a month after Perez had joined Kodak, the two sides announced that they would part company.

But Phogenix wasn't all for naught. Perez had hired two former top HP printer executives, Bill Lloyd and Philip S. Faraci, to help him evaluate the consumer inkjet business for Kodak. In 1979, Lloyd had led the HP team that came up with the key advance in inkjet printing that created the industry. As soon as the Phogenix news came down, Lloyd and Faraci were on the phone with about 40 key employees, many of them former HPers. They couldn't talk about Perez's ambitions yet, but "we called them up and asked them not to take other jobs," recalls Lloyd, who is now Kodak's chief technology officer.

The crucial go/no-go meeting came on June 25, 2003, in Perez's conference room on the nineteenth floor of Kodak headquarters. Lloyd and Faraci laid out the arguments, pro and con. The risks were enormous. Kodak would be entering a mature business that was already dominated by a handful of leaders. And with Kodak's turnaround in question, Perez couldn't afford an expensive failure. But the rewards were huge, too.

Perez decided to sleep on it. He tossed fitfully all night at his home in the posh Pittsford neighborhood of Rochester. By morning, he had made his decision. "The industry had been doing things the same way for 20 years, and it was time for a change," he says. "I called up Bill Lloyd and said: 'Go ahead. Let's launch a full program.'"

A few days later, a dozen former Phogenix employees were invited to lunch at the suburban San Diego home of David Clark, who had been the Phogenix R&D chief. They sat by Clark's backyard pool with a view of the rugged Poway Hills in the distance, munched on chicken salad, and listened raptly while Clark laid out Perez's audacious plan. "At first we thought it was a far stretch. We know how capable HP is and how much technology it has and how much money it spends," recalls Susan H. Tousi, a 10-year HP veteran who now runs R&D for Kodak's inkjet business. Still, within a few days, all but one of those who had sat by Clark's pool decided to sign on. Tousi did so because she liked the start-up mentality and wanted to keep working with people who had become close friends.

Perez wanted to get to market quickly, with a target of three years, so the InkJet Products Group leaders made choices designed to speed up the development process. They worked with technology partners, such as chip-design specialist SigmaTel Inc., rather than trying to design everything from scratch. And once they had established their market goals in late 2003, they never swerved from them. The result: a process that took years less than it might have and required just a $300 million investment.

One of the key decisions was choosing pigment rather than the usual dye as the basis for Kodak's ink. Pigment-based inks hold their colors longer, but typically the colors aren't as vivid. So Kodak engineers had to come up with innovations in ink chemistry, nozzle technology, and paper to produce vivid colors that would also last. Software in the printer evaluates each image and determines what's in it (faces, trees, sky), optimizing the process based on that analysis.

FORMULA CHANGE
Ink is boiled and sprayed through 3,840 nozzles at a rate of 24,000 drops per second. The tiny pigment particles are

designed to sit on the surface of porous paper while the liquid they're suspended in is absorbed. Drying takes just 15 milliseconds, so there are no worries about smearing the prints, which take 28 seconds to produce.

With any new technology, there are invariably glitches. The team faced a near-disaster a year ago when it discovered that the pigment particles in the inks were settling at the bottom of the storage containers, like sediment in a wine bottle. Unless the situation was remedied, image quality would suffer. The problem came fairly late in the development process; the team had already "frozen" the ink formula so that it could design other components of the printer to go with it.

The temptation was to try to fix things without changing the ink recipe. The scientists considered putting a small mechanical mixer in the storage tank. But in the end they decided that doing anything other than reformulate the ink was too risky. That led to a day-and-night work marathon. A month later, the team had its answer: milling the pigment particles much smaller, so that they would stay suspended in liquid. The formula was set, and Tousi came up with a new motto: "Don't dink with the ink."

POWER MOVE

One way to bring a new product to market quickly, as Kodak has done, is to work with experienced partners, rather than trying to create everything from scratch.

Throughout the whole process, Tousi was the stickler for quality. Dubbed "Queen of the Geeks" by her employees, Tousi carries a loupe for magnifying photographs practically everywhere she goes. She even takes prints into the parking lot to study them under harsh sunlight. Time and again, Tousi sent engineers back to the drawing board because their results weren't up to her standards.

Last June, it was Tousi who had to tell Perez that they weren't going to be able to begin marketing the printers for last year's holiday shopping season. She thought more tests were necessary to ensure the highest print quality. In an effort to boost the team's morale, Perez flew to San Diego to meet with the entire engineering staff. He stood on a table so that he could see over their cubicle partitions. He recalls telling them: "Slipping by a quarter doesn't matter that much, but you have to promise me that these printers will work perfectly. We have only one chance to do this right. If our first introduction fails, we fail."

Analysts who have seen Kodak's printers have come away impressed. "The print quality is really good. They're at least as good as everybody else," says Larry Jamieson, director of industry watcher Lyra Research Inc.

POWER MOVE

If Kodak's bet pays off, it will be in large part because it kept to its goal of creating a printer that made more vivid, longer-lasting prints. It resisted shortcuts that would affect quality.

But Perez and Kodak are challenging a giant competitor that has a 33 percent worldwide market share and a sterling reputation among PC and digital-camera users. HP not only gets prime merchandising spots for its printers and ink in stores, but also gets to display its printers in the computer sections because it bundles printers with its PCs. "HP has a lot of customer loyalty. They build a great product. The printers don't break," says analyst Alyson Frasco of market researcher Interactive Data Corp.

It's up to Perez and Kodak to show that they have a truly game-changing product. Perez seems immune to negative thoughts. He tells a story that shows just how confident he is of success. "J. Paul Getty said you have to do just three things to be successful: get up early, work hard, and strike oil," says Perez. "I didn't strike oil in my career, but I did strike ink."

MONDAY MORNING...

THE PROBLEM
Transforming a company whose main business is shrinking

Directly challenging a company with a reputation for excellence that dominates the industry

THE SOLUTION
Develop a cash cushion by selling off ancillary businesses.

Analyze competitors' weaknesses and create a superior product that will excel in areas where others falter.

Boost the company's bottom line by aggressively developing a portfolio of products and services that fit into the organization's larger mission.

Win consumer confidence by making sure that the company's new signature product is of top quality. Hold employees and their work to the highest standards.

Be willing to challenge the conventional wisdom and rethink even longstanding organizational practices.

SUSTAINING THE WIN
Keep the company competitive by embracing a start-up mentality, constantly generating new ideas and working quickly to bring them to market.

ANTONIO M. PEREZ

9

JODY THOMPSON AND CALI RESSLER: NO SCHEDULES, NO MEETINGS, NO JOKE AT BEST BUY

POWER PLAYERS

Best Buy is smashing the clock with no mandatory meetings. This profile looks inside Best Buy's radical reshaping of the workplace and its model for management innovation.

Boost morale and reduce turnover by untethering employees from their desks and allowing them to work where and when they wish.

Develop a results-oriented culture by evaluating employees based on their performance, rather than on the number of hours logged at their desks.

Adopt a meetings-are-optional credo to maximize productivity and efficiency.

Michelle Conlin's cover story on Best Buy appeared in December 2006.

LIFE-WORK BALANCE

One afternoon last year, Chap Achen, who oversees online orders at Best Buy Co., shut down his computer, stood up from his desk, and announced that he was leaving for the day. It was around 2 p.m., and most of Achen's staff were slumped over their keyboards, deep in a post-lunch, LCD-lit trance. "See you tomorrow," said Achen. "I'm going to a matinee."

Under normal circumstances, an early-afternoon departure would have been totally un-Achen. After all, this was a 37-year-old corporate comer whose wife laughs in his face when he utters the words "work-life balance." But at Best Buy's Minneapolis headquarters, similar incidents of strangeness were breaking out all over the ultramodern campus. In employee relations, Steve Hance had suddenly started going hunting on workdays, a Remington 12-gauge in one hand, a Verizon LG in the other. In the retail training department, e-learning specialist Mark Wells was spending his days bombing around the country following rocker Dave Matthews. Single mother Kelly McDevitt, an online promotions manager, started leaving at 2:30 p.m. to pick up her 11-year-old son Calvin from school. Scott Jauman, a Six Sigma black belt, began spending a third of his time at his Northwoods cabin.

At most companies, going AWOL during daylight hours would be grounds for a pink slip. Not at Best Buy. The nation's leading electronics retailer has embarked on a radical— if risky—experiment to transform a culture once known for killer hours and herd-riding bosses. The endeavor, called ROWE, for "results-only work environment," seeks to demolish decades-old business dogma that equates physical presence with productivity. The goal at Best Buy is to judge performance on output instead of hours.

Hence workers pulling into the company's amenity-packed headquarters at 2 p.m. aren't considered late. Nor are those pulling out at 2 p.m. seen as leaving early. There are no schedules. No mandatory meetings. No impression-management hustles. Work is no longer a place where you go, but something you do. It's O.K. to take conference calls while you hunt, collaborate from your lakeside cabin, or log on after dinner so that you can spend the afternoon with your kid.

Best Buy did not invent the postgeographic office. Tech companies have been going bedouin for several years. At IBM, 40 percent of the workforce has no official office; at AT&T, a third of the managers are untethered. Sun Microsystems Inc. calculates that it's saved $400 million in real estate costs over six years by allowing nearly half of all employees to work anywhere they want. And this trend seems to have legs. A recent Boston Consulting Group study found that 85 percent of executives expect a big rise in the number of unleashed workers over the next five years. In fact, at many companies, the most innovative new product may be the structure of the workplace itself.

But arguably no big business has smashed the clock quite as resolutely as Best Buy. The official policy for this post-face-time, location-agnostic way of working is that people are free to work wherever they want, whenever they want, as long as they get their work done. "This is like TiVo for your work," says the program's cofounder, Jody Thompson. By the end of 2007, all 4,000 staffers working at corporate headquarters will be on ROWE. Starting in February, the new work environment will become an official part of Best Buy's recruiting pitch as well as its orientation for new hires. And the company plans to take its clockless campaign to its stores— a high-stakes challenge that no company has tried before in a retail environment.

> POWER MOVE
>
> Employers are discovering that "unleashing" employees doesn't just increase employee output and satisfaction. It also saves big money in real estate costs.

Another thing about this experiment: it wasn't imposed from the top down. It began as a covert guerrilla action that spread virally and eventually became a revolution. The operation was so secret that chief executive Brad Anderson only learned the details two years after the program began transforming his company. Such bottom-up, stealth innovation is exactly the kind of thing Anderson encourages. The Best Buy chief aims to keep innovating

Regardless of the merits of their ideas, change agents should expect to have to fight dirty looks and doubters. While some were quick to jump on Best Buy's new approach, others saw it as threatening and even tried to sabotage it.

even when something is ostensibly working. "ROWE was an idea born and nurtured by a handful of passionate employees," he says. "It wasn't created as the result of some edict."

So bullish are Anderson and his team on the idea that they have formed a subsidiary called CultureRx, set up to help other companies go clockless. CultureRx expects to sign up at least one large client in the coming months.

The CEO may have bought in, but there has been plenty of opposition inside the company. Many executives wondered if the program was simply flextime in a prettier bottle. Others felt that working off-site would lead to longer hours and destroy forever the demarcation between work and personal time. Cynics thought it was all a PR stunt dreamed up by Machiavellian operatives in human resources. And as ROWE infected one department after another, its supporters ran into old-guard saboteurs, who continue to plot an overthrow and spread warnings of a coming paradise for slackers.

Then again, the new work structure's proponents say it's helping Best Buy overcome challenges. And thanks to early successes, some of the program's harshest critics have become true believers. With gross margins on electronics under pressure, and Wal-Mart Stores Inc. and Target Corp. shouldering into Best Buy territory, the company has been moving into services, including its Geek Squad and its "customer-centricity" program in which salespeople act as technology counselors. But Best Buy was afflicted by stress, burnout, and high turnover. The hope was that ROWE, by freeing employees to make their own work-life decisions, could boost morale and productivity and keep the service initiative on track.

It seems to be working. Since the program's implementation, average voluntary turnover has fallen drastically, CultureRx says. Meanwhile, Best Buy notes that productivity is up an average of

35 percent in departments that have switched to ROWE. Employee engagement, which measures employee satisfaction and is often a barometer for retention, is way up too, according to the Gallup Organization, which audits corporate cultures.

ROWE may also help the company pay for the customer-centricity campaign. The endeavor is hugely expensive because it involves tailoring stores to local markets and training employees to turn customer feedback into new business ideas. By letting people work off-campus, Best Buy figures that it can reduce the need for corporate office space, perhaps rent out the empty cubicles to other companies, and plow the millions of dollars in savings into its services initiative.

Phyllis Moen, a University of Minnesota sociology professor who researches work-life issues, is studying the Best Buy experiment in a project sponsored by the National Institutes of Health. She says that most companies are stuck in the 1930s when it comes to employees' and managers' relationships to time and work. "Our whole notion of paid work was developed within an assembly-line culture," Moen says. "Showing up was work. Best Buy is recognizing that sitting in a chair is no longer working."

> **POWER MOVE**
>
> Many companies have found that their work-family programs failed because they had rigid rules that didn't adapt to employees' lives and because perks, like telecommuting schedules, were reserved for just a favored few.

ONE GIANT WIRELESS KIBBUTZ

Jody Thompson and Cali Ressler are two HR people you actually don't hate. They groan over cultish corporate slogans like "Build Superior Organizational Capability." They disdain Outlook junkies who double-book and showboating PowerPointers. But it's flextime, or Big Business's answer to overwork, long commutes, and lack of work-family balance, that elicits the harshest verdict. "A con game," says Thompson. "A total joke," adds Ressler.

Flexible work schedules, they say, heap needless bureaucracy on managers instead of addressing the real issue: how to work more efficiently in an era of transcontinental teams and multiple time zones. They add that flextime also stigmatizes those who use it (the reason that so few do) and keeps companies acting like the military (fixated on schedules) when they should behave more like MySpace (social networks where real-time innovation can flourish). Besides, they say, if people can virtually carry their office around in their pockets or pocketbooks, why should it matter where and when they work if they are crushing their goals?

POWER MOVE

As more people are expected to be collaborating in cross-country teams, some experts believe that the whole notion of face time will become obsolete. Workplaces will operate much more efficiently if they operate more like social networks.

Thompson, 49, and Ressler, 29, met three years ago. The boomer and the Gen Xer got each other right away. When they talk about their meeting, it sounds like something out of *Plato for HR*, or two like minds making a whole. At the time, Best Buy was still a ferociously face-time place. Workers arriving after 8 a.m. on subzero mornings would stash their parkas in their cars to foil detection as late arrivals. Early escapees crept down back stairwells. Cube-side, the living was equally uneasy. One manager required his MBAs to sign out for lunch, including listing their restaurant locations and ETAs. Another insisted that his team track its work—every 15 minutes. As at many companies, the last one to turn out the lights won.

Outside the office, Thompson and Ressler couldn't help noticing how wireless broadband was turning the world into one giant work kibbutz. They talked about how managers were mired in analog-age inertia, often judging performance on how much they saw you, rather than on how much you did. Ressler and Thompson recognized the dangerous, life-wrecking cocktail in the making: the always-on worker now also had to be always in.

The culture, not exactly Minnesota-nice, was threatening Best Buy's massive expansion plans. But Ressler and Thompson knew that their solution was too radical to simply trot up to CEO Anderson. Nor, in the beginning, did they feel that they could lobby their executive supervisors for official approval. Besides, they knew that the usual corporate route of imposing something from the top down would bomb. So they met in private, stealthily strategizing about how to protect ROWE and then dribble it out under the radar in tiny pilot trials. Ressler and Thompson waited patiently for the right opportunity.

It came in 2003. Two managers—one in the properties division, the other in communications—were desperate. Their top performers were complaining of unsustainable levels of stress, threatening business continuity just when Best Buy was rolling out its customer-centricity campaign in hundreds of stores. They also knew from employee engagement data that workers were suffering from the classic work-life hex: jobs with high demands (always-on, transcontinental availability) and low control (always on-site, no personal life).

Ressler and Thompson saw their opening in these two vanguard managers. Would they be willing to take part in a private management experiment? The two outlined their vision. They explained how in the world of ROWE, there would be no mandatory meetings. No times when you had to physically be at work. Performance would be based on output, not hours. Managers would base their assessments on data and evidence, not feelings and anecdotes. The executives liked what they heard and agreed.

POWER MOVE

Overcoming opposition to a new proposal can sometimes be as simple as sharing the numbers. When one Best Buy executive saw the data showing that teams using ROWE were processing more orders and felt better about their jobs, he became an evangelist for the program.

The experiment quickly gained social networking heat. Waiting in line at Best Buy's on-site Caribou Coffee, in e-mails, and during drive-bys at friends' desks, employees in other parts of the company started hearing about this seeming antidote to megahour agita. A curious culture of haves and have-nots emerged on the Best Buy campus, with those in ROWE sporting special stickers on their laptops as

> **POWER MOVE**
>
> When workers are free to be nomads, regular gatherings, in person or by videoconference, help to retain a team dynamic.

though they were part of some cabal. Hance, the hunter, started taking conference calls in tree stands and exchanging e-mails from his fishing boat. When Wells wasn't following Dave Matthews around, chances were that he was biking around Minneapolis's network of urban lakes, digging into work only after night had fallen. Hourly workers were still putting in a full 40, but they began doing so wherever and whenever they wanted.

At first, participants were loath to share anything about ROWE with higher-ups for fear that the perk would be taken away or reversed. But by 2004, loftier and loftier levels of management began hearing about the experiment, and at about the same time, opposition to it grew more intense. Critics feared that executives would lose control and that coworkers would forfeit the collaboration born of proximity. If you can work anywhere, they asked, won't you always be working? Won't overbearing bosses start calling you in the middle of the night? Won't coasters see ROWE as a way to shirk work and force more dedicated colleagues to pick up the slack? And there were generational conflicts: some boomers felt they'd been forced to choose between work and life during their careers. So everyone else should, too.

Shari Ballard, Best Buy's executive vice president for human capital and leadership (an analog title if ever there was one), was originally skeptical, although she eventually bought in. At first she couldn't figure out why managers needed a new methodology to help solve the work-life conundrum. "It wasn't hugs and smiles," she says of Ressler's and Thompson's campaign. "Managers in the old mental model were totally irritated." In the e-learning division, many of Wells's older coworkers (read 40-year-olds; the average age at Best Buy is 36) expressed resentment over the change, insisting that work relationships are better face-to-face, not screen-to-screen. "We have people in our group who are like, `I'm not going to do it,'" says Wells, who likes to sleep in and doesn't own an alarm clock. "I'm like, `That's fine, but I'm outta here.'" In enemy circles, Ressler and Thompson are known to this day as "those two" and "the subversives."

Yet ROWE continues to spread through the company. If intrigued nonparticipants work for progressive superiors, they usually talk up the program and get their bosses to agree to trials. If they toil under clock-watchers, they form underground networks and quietly lobby for outside support until their boss usually has no choice but to switch. It was only this past summer that CEO Anderson got a full briefing, and total understanding, about what was happening. "We purposely waited until the tipping point before we took it to him," says Thompson. Until then, he wasn't well versed on the 13 ROWE commandments. No.1: People at all levels stop doing any activity that is a waste of their time, the customer's time, or the company's money. No.7: Nobody talks about how many hours they work. No.9: It's O.K. to take a nap on a Tuesday afternoon, grocery shop on Wednesday morning, or catch a movie on Thursday afternoon.

That's the commandment Achen was following when he took off that day to see *Star Wars Episode III: Revenge of the Sith*. Doing so felt abnormal and uncomfortable. Achen felt guilty. But Ressler and Thompson had told him to "model the behavior." So he did. It helped that Achen saw ROWE as having the potential to solve a couple of nagging business problems. As the head of the unit that monitors everything that happens after someone places an order at BestBuy.com, including manually reviewing orders and flagging them for possible fraud, Achen wanted to expand the hours of operation without mandating that people show up in the office at 6 a.m. He also had another issue: one of his top-performing managers lived in St. Cloud, Minnesota, and commuted two and a half hours each

POWER MOVE

Location-agnostic work is a difficult concept to grasp. Thus, employees participating in ROWE are given a list of 13 commandments that serves as a guide and manifesto for the program.

way to work. He and Achen had a gentleman's agreement that he could work from home on Fridays. But the rest of the staff didn't appreciate the favoritism. "It was creating a lot of tension on my team," says Achen.

POWER MOVE

Perhaps one of the biggest time wasters in the corporate world is meetings. To avoid that pitfall, Best Buy managers treat meetings as a last resort, rather than as a sign of good management.

RECORD JOB SATISFACTION

Ressler and Thompson had convinced Achen that ROWE would work. Now Achen would have to convince the general manager of BestBuy.com, senior vice president John "J.T." Thompson. That wasn't going to be easy. Thompson, a former General Electric Co. guy, was as old school as they come, with his starched shirt, booming voice, and ramrod-straight posture. He came of age believing that there were three 8-hour days in every 24 hours. He loved working in his office on weekends. At first, he pushed back hard. "I was not supportive," says Thompson, who was privately terrified about the loss of control. "He didn't want anything to do with it," says Achen. "He was all about measurement, and he kept asking me, `How are you going to measure this so you know you're getting the same productivity out of people?'"

That's where Achen's performance metrics came in handy. He could measure how many orders per hour his team was processing no matter where they were. He told Thompson he'd reel everyone back to campus the minute he noticed a dip. Within a month, Achen could see that not only was his team's productivity up, but engagement scores, or measures of job satisfaction and retention, were the highest in the dot-com division's history.

For years, engagement had been a sore spot for Thompson. "I showed J.T. these scores, and his eyes lit up," says Achen. Thompson rushed to roll out ROWE to his entire department. Voluntary turnover among men dropped from 16.11 percent to 0. "For years I had been focused on the wrong currency," says Thompson. "I was always looking to see if people were here. I should have been looking at what they were getting done."

Today, Achen's commuting employee usually comes in once a week. Nearly three-quarters of his staff spend most of their time out of the office. Doesn't he worry that he loses some of the interoffice magic when people don't gather together all day, every day? What about the value of riffing on one another's ideas? What about teamwork and camaraderie? "You absolutely lose some of that," he says. "But what we get back far outweighs anything we've lost."

Achen says he would never go back. Orders processed by people who are not working in the office are up 13 to 18 percent over those processed by people who are. ROWEers are posting higher metrics for quality, too. Achen says he believes that's due to the new office paradox: given the constant distractions, it sometimes feels impossible to get any work done at work.

Ressler and Thompson say that all the Best Buy groups that have switched to the freer structure are reporting similar results. Meanwhile, the two have other big plans for the company. Last month they launched a new pilot called Cube-Free. Ressler and Thompson believe that offices encourage the wrong kinds of habits, keeping people wrapped up in a paper, prewireless mentality as opposed to pushing employees to use technology in the efficiency-enhancing way that was intended. Offices also waste space and time in an age when workers are becoming more and more place-neutral. "This also sets up Best Buy to be able to completely operate if disaster hits," says Thompson. Work groups that go cube-free will be able to redesign their spaces to better accommodate collaboration instead of working alone.

Next year Ressler and Thompson plan to pilot their boldest move yet, testing ROWE among both managers and workers in

> **POWER MOVE**
>
> One way to win acceptance of a new program is to let it spread on its own. Instead of dictating that managers implement ROWE, Best Buy executives quietly encouraged a few eager workers to try it, and soon more volunteered.

retail stores. How exactly they will do this in an environment where salespeople presumably need to put in regular hours, they won't say. And they acknowledge that it won't be easy. Still, they are eager to try just about anything to help the company slash its 65 percent turnover rates in stores, where disgruntlement is common and workers form groups on MySpace with names like "Best Buy Losers Club!"

Best Buy has transformed its workplace culture in a remarkably short time. Isn't it also true that ROWE could unravel just as quickly? What happens if the company hits a speed bump? Competition isn't getting any less intense, after all. Best Buy sells a lot of extended warranties, an area where both Wal-Mart and Target are eager to undercut the electronics retailer on price. What's more, the current boom in flat-panel digital TVs will peak in a few years.

If Best Buy's business goes south, human nature dictates that the people who always believed that the clockless office was a flaky New Age idea will see an opportunity to try to force a hasty retreat. Some at the company complain that productivity is up only because many Best Buyers are now working longer hours. And some die-hard ROWE opponents still privately roll their eyes when they see Ressler and Thompson in the hallway.

But it's worth remembering that most big companies fail to grow at the rate of inflation. That's true in part because the bigger the company gets, the harder it is to get the best out of each and every employee. ROWE is one of Best Buy's answers to avoiding that fate. "The old way of managing and looking at work isn't going to work anymore," says Ressler. "We want to revolutionize the way work gets done." Admit it, you're rooting for them, too.

THE PROBLEM

Giving employees the freedom to structure their work to meet their own needs, while also improving the bottom line

Thoroughly transforming the corporate culture so that people learn to work differently

THE SOLUTION

Conduct an under-the-radar campaign. Let support build organically, rather than trying to force the new culture on employees.

Make sure that the early adopters lead by example and serve as positive role models.

Closely track the metrics after unplugging workers, to ensure that productivity, engagement, and turnover improve.

Work hard to preserve camaraderie and fight isolation by organizing get-togethers.

SUSTAINING THE WIN

Continue to remake the culture by spreading it into new corners of the company, but be careful to use a soft touch so as to avoid a backlash.

JODY THOMPSON and CALI RESSLER

J ALLARD:
THE SOUL OF A NEW MICROSOFT

POWER PLAYER
Edgy thinkers like J Allard are looking far beyond Windows for the next big thing at Microsoft.

This December 2006 cover story profile is by Jay Greene with Peter Burrows.

LESSON PLAN

Transform a lumbering, bureaucratic giant into a nimble competitor so that it can adapt to a fast-changing industry.

Keep the company growing by expanding aggressively into new markets and developing value-added products and services.

Stay ahead of the competition by cultivating a new crop of leaders who will inspire out-of-the-box thinking.

TASTE OF MICROSOFT

At 3:32 p.m. on October 19, an e-mail flashed across the screens of the 230 Microsoft employees working slavishly to bring the Zune music player to market. The sender was their brash team leader, J Allard, 37. The message included a link to an old video of Steve Jobs on YouTube, mocking Microsoft's creativity. "The only problem with Microsoft is that they have no taste," the Apple Computer boss says. "They have absolutely no taste."

Allard was using one of the oldest motivational tricks in the book—his version of a football coach posting an opponent's quote on the locker room wall. "I for one . . . want to see this guy eat his words," Allard wrote. "Those are fighting words. He is speaking to every one of us and saying that we don't get it."

Zune hit store shelves on November 14—a mere eight months after Allard's team got the go-ahead for the seemingly impossible task of toppling Apple's iPod music player. Contrast that with the five years and some 10,000 Microsoft Corp. workers it took to give birth to the latest version of the company's Windows operating system, Vista, which begins selling to corporate customers on November 30 (and to consumers in January). From the start, Vista has seemed like an anachronism—packaged software in a Web 2.0 era where ever more applications are moving off the PC and onto the Internet, some springing forth in a matter of weeks. Microsoft chief executive Steven A. Ballmer vows that this time-consuming process of cranking out code, which created complexity and bogged down development, will never be repeated.

No one's suggesting that Zune will have anywhere near the impact of Vista. In its early form, it is clearly no iPod killer. It's bulkier and more of a battery hog, and the Zune marketplace doesn't offer as many songs or videos as Apple Computer Inc.'s iTunes does. Plus, you pay for

> **POWER MOVE**
>
> One surefire way to motivate and rally the ranks is to remind them of their competitor's taunts. Allard, for instance, sent his Zune staffers a video of Steve Jobs belittling Microsoft's taste.

those songs or videos with a confusing point system instead of dollars and cents. Zune will be lucky to sell 3 million units its first year and is sure to lose money for the foreseeable future. Vista, on the other hand, should run on about 76 million PCs by the end of 2007, says Roger Kay, founder of research firm Endpoint Technologies Associates. Vista sales should help fuel an $11.5 billion contribution to operating profits from Windows in the current fiscal year, says Credit Suisse First Boston analyst Jason Maynard.

> **POWER MOVE**
>
> To change the mindset of an organization as massive as Microsoft, the people at the top have to be willing to let creative thinkers challenge the status quo and undertake risky new projects.

But maybe the point is that Microsoft needs to find its un-Vista. Several of them, in fact. The software giant is entering perhaps the greatest upheaval in its 30-year history. New business models are emerging—from low-cost "open-source" software to advertising-supported Web services—that threaten Microsoft's core business like never before. If investors are to care about the company, it needs to find new growth markets. Its $44.3 billion in annual sales is puttering along at an 11 percent growth pace. Its shares, which soared 9,560 percent throughout the 1990s, sank 63 percent in 2000 when the Internet bubble burst, and they have yet to fully recover.

Reigniting growth will require a cultural shift at a company that has long shaped its strategy around maintaining its Windows operating system and Office word processing and spreadsheet monopolies. That calls for a new breed of leaders who can push the company in directions it hasn't gone before. "Things are different from the desktop world that most of the Microsoft guys grew up in," says Michael A. Cusumano, a management professor at Massachusetts Institute of Technology who has written extensively about the company.

No one leader will replace William H. Gates III, the iconic software geek who came to define an era and who plans to leave the company in June 2008. But a cadre of executives is positioned to step up. Steven Sinofsky, the longtime head of the Office unit and onetime Gates technical assistant, has been put in charge of speeding up the Windows product cycle. Ray Ozzie, a relative Microsoft newbie and computing industry icon, is working to Webify many of Microsoft's products.

The soul of the new Microsoft, though—its Geek 2.0—may just be Allard, the vice president for design and development at its Entertainment & Devices unit. Allard looks and acts nothing like the prototypical Microsofty. Over the years, he's swapped his plaid shirt and khakis—something of a Microsoft uniform—for edgy jackets made by Mark Ecko and other designer wear. He loads up his nine iPods, and now his Zune, with songs from hard-core bands like A.R.E. Weapons. And he's a downhill mountain biking maniac who has broken several bones after flying off his bike.

More important than his cool quotient, though, is that Allard gets things done—fast. Zune is only the latest example. At the turn of the decade, he led the software giant into the video game business with Xbox, a risky gambit that's just starting to pay off. Xbox is now a solid number two to Sony Corp.'s PlayStation, and analysts expect it to turn its first profit in the next fiscal year.

Allard is one of more than 100 Microsoft vice presidents, but he has played an outsized role in shifting perceptions about whether the company can innovate in areas other than packaged software. In June, when Gates announced his plan to focus on his charitable foundation full time, he anointed Allard, along with a handful of others, as one of the leaders he expects to clear new paths.

Already, Allard and those like him are having an impact. They're showing that strategies to move the company beyond Windows can emerge and be accepted by top brass as nonthreatening. A key moment came six years ago, when Allard insisted that the new Xbox video game console be developed without using Windows. In one meeting, Gates berated him for suggesting that the operating system wasn't up to snuff. But Allard argued that it wasn't specialized enough to handle video gaming. Gates eventually relented, a decision that is widely seen today as a key to the console's success.

Even Ballmer, once pigeonholed as a micromanager, seems increasingly willing to distribute power and let those underneath him try new approaches. "I would have been hell-bent and determined six years ago to call Xbox the Windows Game Machine," he says. "My natural tendency would have been to call Zune something that was related to Xbox, since we had some consumer franchise. And yet we're really building consumer marketing muscle, and those guys are really teaching and educating us on new ways to do things."

Never afraid to speak his mind, Allard started pushing buttons way back in 1994, when, as an eager 25-year-old programmer who had been on Microsoft's payroll only three years, he penned a sea-changing memo titled "Windows: The Next Killer Application on the Internet," which found its way to Gates. The note, now part of Microsoft lore, helped awaken Gates to the potential and threat of the Web. "I'm a pain-in-the-ass change agent," Allard says.

That's exactly what Microsoft needs if it hopes to again set the tech agenda. Windows and Office will deliver more revenues in coming years than the exports of many small nations. But Web spitfires such as Google Inc. and Salesforce.com have the wind at their backs. And while Microsoft continues to recruit top talent, it also continues to see key leaders move on: executives such as Vic Gundotra, a top evangelist in its developer division, who will soon join Google, and Brian Valentine, the longtime leader of the Windows server business, who now works for Amazon.com Inc.

Nowhere are Microsoft's missteps more apparent than in digital music. When that business first emerged five years ago, the company saw it through Windows-colored glasses. Using the same model that worked in PCs, Microsoft produced software to play music on computers and handheld devices, slapped the Windows brand on it, and left the hardware design to partners. Microsoft figured that Apple was making the same mistake with the iPod that it had made with its Macintosh PCs:

by creating both the proprietary hardware and the software, it would lock out partners and limit growth.

But it turns out that the silky experience of hardware married inextricably with software was crucial in coaxing nontechies into the world of digital music and downloading. Microsoft's market share pales in comparison with Apple's because its software never worked smoothly with devices that came from partners such as Creative Labs and with services from outfits like MTV. Apple seized 85 percent of the song download business and to date has sold 67 million devices and 1.5 billion songs.

POWER MOVE

If a company wants to challenge a product as well-designed and iconic as the iPod, it can't simply create a pale imitation. It has to break new ground. So Zune is the first MP3 player to offer Wi-Fi capabilities.

When Allard's team hatched Zune, it unabashedly cribbed from Apple's playbook. Microsoft all but abandoned its music partners, built its own device, and offered its own music-selling service. Moreover, the player and the service, which work exclusively with each other, operate far more smoothly than any previous iPod challenger.

Allard recognizes, though, that he can't beat Apple merely by mimicking its best features. So he wants to change the rules of the game. That's why he led the effort to include wireless fidelity, or Wi-Fi, inside Zune. Zunesters can use it to beam songs to friends' devices. Microsoft cut deals with record studios, persuading them to let consumers share music in a tolerable way; Zune includes technology that limits beamed songs to three plays or three days, whichever comes first. Labels bought into the idea of promotion. "My customer becomes your street team," Allard says.

Microsoft is betting that Zune will follow the path of Xbox. Like the game machine, Zune arrives as a flawed first version that screams for an update. And like a much-criticized networking feature on Xbox that eventually gave it an edge when online gaming took off, Zune's Wi-Fi technology hints at a broader vision.

Sitting in the open, communal meeting space at the center of Zune headquarters—a refurbished dance studio a few miles from the main Microsoft campus—Allard wonders why every pundit is so focused on the device rather than the listening experience. He envisions a time (not soon, mind you) when all of your music will be "in the cloud"—tech-speak for Net-connected servers that dish up content wherever you happen to be, beamed to any device. Hop on a plane, plug headphones into the armrest, and poof!—there's your music. Set your hotel alarm clock to wake you to your favorite song. Zune may be a swell device, but for Allard it's a means to a much larger end.

The giant of Redmond is starting to take an Allard-like fresh look at many of its older product lines as well. Webification can be seen seeping into all corners of its Redmond (Washington) headquarters. Its leading proponent is Ozzie, who developed Lotus Notes in the 1980s, then joined Microsoft in 2005 when it acquired his Groove Networks. Ozzie quickly emerged as heir to Gates's role as technology sage. Under the year-old "Live" strategy, Microsoft is blending services that it launches on the Web with programs that consumers run on their PCs. That way, Netizens get a better experience using Web services when they harness Windows and the processing power of PCs. Take Windows Live Mail, a small software program that lets users view various e-mail accounts—even Google's Gmail— in the same window. Because it runs on a PC desktop, it's easy to include zippy features such as automatically completing an e-mail address after you type in a few keystrokes. Microsoft will give away services such as e-mail, limited Web hosting, and perhaps one day that portable jukebox in the sky that Allard dreams of, making money from advertising and subscriptions.

POWER MOVE

Sometimes large companies have to learn to think small. The reason why Microsoft took too much time—more than five years— to release Vista was because its goals were too big. It has learned to downsize its ambitions.

Challenging Google on the Web and Apple in music are stretches for a company that critics say lacks a culture of innovation. But while nearly all the company's profits come from the old products, the growth opportunities are in the businesses that Allard and Ozzie are igniting. Xbox, for example, should ring up $4.6 billion in sales in the fiscal year that ends next June, says Goldman Sachs & Co. analyst Rick Sherlund. That number should climb 67 percent, to $7.6 billion, in fiscal 2009. He estimates that Zune sales will climb from $250 million to $575 million over the same period. By that time he expects the Home & Entertainment unit, which includes Xbox and Zune, to kick in $1.2 billion in operating profits.

Lately, some outsiders who work with Microsoft are detecting signs that the culture is slowly shifting as well. "They're definitely in the middle of a strategy relook," says Hewlett-Packard Co. chief strategy and technical officer Shane V. Robison, who chats with Microsoft brass. "It will be a fairly orderly evolution, but there's a lot of new discussion that I'm seeing."

There's hardly anything old school about Allard. On a drizzly fall night in the Seattle suburb of Issaquah, he sets out with some Microsoft mountain biking buddies for a ride through a pitch-black forest. Guided only by lights mounted to their helmets and handlebars, the group bumps over tree roots, splashes through puddles, and powers over trails, some no more than two feet wide. Allard hustles his bike up yet another hill, then stops to catch his breath and check his heart-rate monitor. It's racing high, at 197 beats per minute. A minute later he's back in the saddle, looking for the next hill to climb.

With Allard, everything is about velocity. He drives a Ferrari 360 and a Porsche 911. He bombs down ski runs during the summer on a mountain bike at speeds topping 30 miles an hour. He qualified for the U.S. Nationals race this summer but had to drop out after he was hit by a car while biking around Seattle. "I love that gravity is unforgiving," he says. He even blazes through e-mail, jotting down notes all in lowercase: "shift key slows you down," he writes.

His fascination with technology and commerce started early. When Allard was about 12, he wrote an elaborate computer game called Lemonade Stand. The proprietor started with a $5 allowance to buy sugar and lemons. You had to look at weather reports; if you guessed wrong and made too much lemonade, it would go bad and take your investment with it. "If I had half a brain, I would have waited 10 years, called it Sim Lemonade and made a bazillion," Allard jokes.

POWER MOVE

In the Web 2.0 economy, speed is essential. To bring products to market quickly, companies need to be willing to release products that are good enough and then issue updates and corrections as needed.

A B+ student who thrived on math, Allard dove deep into computer engineering at Boston University. He and his future wife, Rebecca Norlander, impressed a Microsoft recruiter enough at an MIT job fair to get two tickets to Seattle for a full round of interviews. (Norlander also works at Microsoft, most recently as general manager of the security business unit.) During one session, Brian Valentine, then a networking manager, asked Allard what he'd want his epitaph to read if he died tomorrow. There was little hesitation: "Go big or go home."

In college, Allard had become addicted to the Internet. Raw as it was back then, he connected to others with similar interests and had an inkling of the power it held to bring together the masses. But Microsoft had no clue. It had registered microsoft.com as an Internet domain name only a few months before Allard landed, more than five years after Sun Microsystems Inc. had registered its name. Microsoft was far more interested in desktop computing than in figuring out how to make all those computers work together.

Three years into his Microsoft tenure, Allard was working on Windows NT server software, with no direct reports. Frustrated, he wrote his now-famous memo. Allard wanted Microsoft to figure out what Internet users wanted to do,

By listening to change agents in its midst, an organization can unleash fresh ideas and reposition itself for a new era. As a 23-year-old, Allard wrote a prescient memo that helped awaken Microsoft to the Internet.

build tools to help them do it, and become a technical leader before rivals did. "Embrace, extend, then innovate," he wrote. "Change the rules: Windows becomes the next-generation Internet tool of the future!"

That message, along with an e-mail to Gates from Sinofsky, served to awaken the slumbering company. Allard became a star, and Microsoft focused on connecting customers through its server and PC software, crushing Web browser pioneer Netscape Communications Corp. along the way.

But the Net and Microsoft were still an awkward fit. In the late 1990s, Allard was put in charge of a wildly elaborate Web-services initiative dubbed Project 42. The group took its name from the cult classic book *The Hitchhiker's Guide to the Galaxy*, in which the absurd answer to the question, "What is the meaning of the universe?" is 42.

Allard now says that he used the name in part because the group's goals seemed equally absurd. Its roster expanded to an unmanageable 1,500 workers, and the project became a clearinghouse for every Web idea that bubbled up. "We started with the organization first, not the dream," Allard recalls. "It was quickly the answer to everything." Team members sparred over different visions for the Web: would it be tightly coupled to Windows or open to other technologies? In May 1999, Project 42 disbanded, collapsing under its own weight.

Microsoft's longtime Windows chief, James E. Allchin, later described the effort as "incredibly ambitious and naive." Allard pondered that barb recently and wondered if it was really a knock. "The only way to change the world is to imagine it different than the way it is today," he says. "Apply too much of the wisdom and knowledge that got us here, and you end up right where you started. Take a fresh look from a new perspective, and get a new result."

Allard took two months off and pondered his next gig. Based on the Project 42 debacle, he knew he had to start small: "The critical lesson was: crawl, walk, run." A handful of buddies working on an idea to build a video game device needed someone with political clout. Allard still had sway with Gates and Ballmer, so he dove in.

Just as in the pre-Internet days, Microsoft was stuck thinking conventionally. Allard's bosses wanted to develop a video game version of Windows and get computer makers, such as Dell Inc., to build the device. But the industry didn't work that way. Hardware makers lose money on console sales and make it back from royalties on games. When it became clear that Microsoft had to enter the console business, building from scratch wasn't his superior's first choice. "I wanted to acquire Nintendo," recalls Rick Thompson, a vice president who then ran the hardware business. Allard pushed to do the whole project in-house, and Microsoft ultimately vaulted ahead of Nintendo.

POWER MOVE

Wildly successful companies like Microsoft are learning that even they can lose traction if they cling to old ways when business models change. So instead of getting partners to build new devices while it supplies the software, as the company has done for years, Microsoft is now creating new gadgets, like Xbox, from scratch.

Allard's reward for the success of Xbox was being put in charge of finding new multibillion-dollar device businesses, which became the quest to topple Apple's iPod. The enemy in this case is very familiar: behind Allard's desk is a crystal given to him by his boss, Microsoft entertainment division president Robert J. Bach, upon his fifteenth anniversary at the company. In the middle sits a photo of Steve Jobs. Always the iconoclast, Allard works on an Apple G5 computer, next to an obviously less frequently used PC. Allard says it's important to learn about the competition.

Allard has surrounded himself with a small posse of loyal colleagues who move with him from project to project. Douglas C. Hebenthal started with Allard 15 years ago on a networking product called LAN Manager. Hebenthal ticks off the big assignments they've shared since: Internet Information Server, Project 42, Xbox, and now Zune. "In every case in which I work with J, there is a mountain to climb, there is a clear leader, and most folks would see that mountain as insurmountable," he says. "The thing about the guys who work with J is that we never think things are insurmountable. In fact, that's the draw."

MONDAY MORNING...

THE PROBLEM
Finding and developing new multibillion-dollar device businesses as the growth of the company's core business slows

THE SOLUTION
Give trailblazing, visionary types the power to launch new ventures that will move the company in new directions.

Be willing to rethink the company's tried-and-true approaches and experiment with new ones.

"Webify" old products to keep them relevant, and make sure new products are future-proofed by giving them Wi-Fi and other networking capabilities.

Speed up the product-development process.

SUSTAINING THE WIN
Keep encouraging the change agents to assume leadership roles by rewarding outspokenness and risk taking.

J ALLARD

JAMIE DIMON:
JPMORGAN'S GRAND DESIGN

POWER PLAYER

In 2005, Jamie Dimon was bracing for another tough year at JPMorgan. This is an inside look at his $1.1 billion plan to revive the nation's number two bank, which offers lessons in strategy innovations.

This story, from March 2005, was reported by Mara Der Hovanesian, with Emily Thornton, Stanley Reed, and Joseph Weber.

Boost productivity by devoting resources to strengthening the organization's technology infrastructure.

Kick-start growth by developing new products and services that will appeal to a wider client base.

Reach new markets by building synergistic partnerships both inside and outside the organization.

Impose financial discipline without stinting on the capital investments needed for long-term growth.

FIRST TO THE PUNCH

One winter night, JPMorgan Chase & Co. pulled out the stops for a lavish bash at New York's American Museum of Natural History. Among the 200 or so guests were such luminaries as Senator Hillary Rodham Clinton (D-N.Y.) and Apple Computer Inc. CEO Steven P. Jobs. It was as much a celebration of the bank as it was a fund-raiser for the Global Fund for Women. After years of consolidation, JPMorgan had amassed more than $1 trillion in assets, only the second U.S. bank ever to get so big. From the podium, Walter V. Shipley, 70, the long-retired chairman of Chase Manhattan Corp., asked rhetorically: "Who here even remembers what the market cap of Manufacturers Hanover was when it merged with Chemical Bank?"—the deal that set the ball rolling toward the creation of JPMorgan Chase 15 years later.

At the head table, banking brainiac Jamie Dimon blurted out the answer: $1.9 billion. It was classic Dimon. JPMorgan's president and chief operating officer is often first to the punch, knows his numbers cold, and is unabashed about making that loud and clear. He also has an uncanny knack for inadvertently upstaging the main event. Dimon spent more than 15 years at Citigroup and its predecessors as right hand to Sanford "Sandy" I. Weill and three years as CEO of Chicago's once-troubled Bank One Corp. The 49-year-old Dimon's obsession with detail and disdain for waste have made him a corporate legend. General Electric Co. had Neutron Jack Welch. JPMorgan has its Hatchet Man.

In the year since the $58.5 billion sale of Bank One to JPMorgan, the boy from Queens and CEO-in-waiting has gone about doing what he does best. By year-end, most of the 12,000 jobs to be cut—about 7 percent of the workforce— will be gone. A $5 billion outsourcing contract with IBM and executive perks such as country club memberships and first-class travel are already history. Yet melding the two banks— each with a legacy of half-digested mergers and chaotic back-office systems—is turning out to be trickier than expected. Since finalizing its merger last July 1, the bank has had two back-to-back quarters of weak earnings, caused by poor trading results, escalating merger costs, and rising wages, mostly in the investment bank.

"TONS OF IDEAS"

What's more, the immediate outlook looks grim. *BusinessWeek* has learned that this year's earnings will be much worse than the $3.06 per share that Wall Street now expects after cutting its estimates by 21 cents in January. Part of the reason is rising legal costs: on March 16, JPMorgan became the last bank to settle a class action over lending to WorldCom for $2 billion. Dimon is rebuilding reserves with $900 million, which will cut first-quarter earnings. Two months ago, he warned analysts that merger costs would rise yet again. Originally estimated at $3 billion, the costs were later revised upward to $4 billion. Then he said they'll balloon to $500 million more. Meantime, annual cost savings will reach only 70 percent of his $3 billion target by the end of the year. Still, he promised that the bank will be in a "fabulous position" by 2006. Says Bank of America securities analyst John E. McDonald: "What some investors saw as a one-to-two-year turnaround now looks more like a three-to-five-year story."

In a series of interviews, Dimon and his team of Citi and Bank One veterans gave *BusinessWeek* an exclusive look at his ambitious growth plan. Primed with $1.1 billion of new spending, on top of $35.5 billion in annual operating expenses, it raises the bar on what he must achieve. That's because it will eat up over half of this year's cost savings. Dimon's strategy reflects three cardinal points of his long-held management philosophy. First, bolster the tech infrastructure to drive efficiency and innovation. Next, invest in businesses that capitalize on strengths, such as consumer finance, debt underwriting,

POWER MOVE

When it comes to controlling costs, Jamie Dimon is ruthless about slashing executive perks like country club memberships and first-class travel. "Cars, phones, clubs, perks—what's that got to do with customers?" he says.

and money management, and rein in those that don't, like auto leasing. Finally, generate more top-line revenue by selling customers a bunch of new products. Says Dimon, who will succeed William B. Harrison, Jr., 61, as CEO next spring: "We've got tons of ideas."

For starters, he'll overhaul the retail bank—from fresh paint to new ATMs. He'll also hire 1,000 salespeople and double, to 14, the number of offices in the Northeast catering strictly to affluent customers with up to $25 million in assets. He will go national, spreading his branch network beyond just 17 states. He'll also go global, opening eight private-bank offices abroad, including the bank's first ever in Japan, where regulatory failures led to Citi's private bank being closed. The investment bank, which Dimon admits "has a long way to go," will get new commodities and currency trading platforms, partly to snag some of the $6 billion in fees that hedge funds pay Wall Street annually. He's also expanding a nascent 401(k) administration business. "What is growth?" says Dimon, in his trademark staccato style. "It's better service, better products, more hours. Growth to me is every budget review. It's 1,000 small steps."

POWER MOVE

Most blue chip companies are aggressively pursuing expansion opportunities abroad. JPMorgan is trying to mine for more business overseas through its joint venture with a respected British financial advisory firm.

Small steps to Dimon, but a giant leap of faith for Wall Street. Some investors fear that Dimon's cost cutting will damage the bank's earning power before new revenues click in. He has sold off $30 billion of Treasury securities that raked in about $1 billion of income a year, along with $6 billion in mobile home and recreational vehicle loans. By selling off these portfolios and stashing away reserves far beyond what either regulators or the bank's own targets require, he is building a "fortress balance sheet" that is capable of weathering rising interest rates and tougher lending markets. Also, he added $3.7 billion to litigation reserves last year, which will be replenished by another $900 million after the bank settles the WorldCom class action.

Despite its size, JPMorgan has no retail brokerage, limited international reach, few dealings with the booming hedge-fund industry, and weak equity underwriting and merger advice businesses. Dimon doesn't intend to get into any business "just to say we're in it." All the same, some analysts worry that he'll get sidetracked into joining a bidding war for brokerages Morgan Stanley or Bear, Stearns & Co. should they be put in play, as some expect.

POWER MOVE

Despite his reputation for thriftiness, Dimon has allocated big money to build sophisticated trading platforms and standardize all the bank's back-office systems. Why? Modernizing the company's infrastructure will help streamline operations.

Although many JPMorgan staffers seem happy to have a young, dynamic banker in charge, rather than the courtly Harrison, some find Dimon's blunt, in-your-face management style grating. Last summer he cut programs that matched gifts to charities and 401(k) contributions for the highest-paid executives, rankling them. "He's going down like cod liver oil," says one JPMorgan investment banker. Still, some suspect that he cultivates a tough-guy image to keep people in line. Tattle about his antics, such as shouting at people or peremptorily firing traders, abounds. "If the rumors aren't true, he certainly doesn't do anything to quash them," says Richard X. Bove, an analyst with Punk, Ziegel & Co.

The competitive pressure is unrelenting. Rivals such as Citi and Bank of America are ahead in going national. Regional players like Commerce Bancorp Inc. and Fifth Third Bancorp are snapping at Dimon's heels in his best markets, New York and Chicago. "They've got all these piranhas nibbling at their core business, and they haven't done anything about it for years," says CreditSights analyst David A. Hendler.

General business conditions won't help Dimon much, either. The move to higher interest rates won't be smooth: mortgage and fixed-income trading—which made up 20 percent of

POWER MOVE

One way to step up sales is to offer more financial incentives to employees. So in addition to opening up 175 new branches, Chase is hiring 1,000 "personal bankers," who, unlike tellers, will earn bonuses for selling home loans and investments.

JPMorgan's $26 billion revenues last year—will take a hit.

Despite the hurdles, many on Wall Street say that Dimon can succeed. They argue that he delivered growth for Weill at Primerica, Smith Barney, Salomon Bros., and Travelers Group. Says Brad Hintz, an analyst at Sanford C. Bernstein & Co.: "He has taken on a major challenge, but I'm making a bet that he has the tenacity and experience to win."

Dimon ran his own show for the first time at Bank One, the nation's sixth-largest bank. A lifelong New Yorker, he moved his wife and three then-school-age girls to the Windy City (he still commutes) in March 2000. The bank had just reported a net loss of $511 million, the result of a mishmash of previous mergers. Dimon lopped off $1.8 billion in costs and one-fifth of the workforce. Cutbacks, he insists, were not his only legacy. In 2003 the bank earned a record $3.5 billion, nabbing a net 434,000 new checking accounts, vs. 4,000 the year before. The same year, credit card sales leaped 83 percent and home equity loans 29 percent.

EYE ON INTEGRATION

As he did at Bank One, Dimon is betting big on information technology. It will get the largest slug of extra cash, $600 million on top of an existing $6.5 billion tech budget. Simply stitching the two banks together is a huge task. Over the next 12 to 18 months, thousands of people will spend more than two million hours on 750 different projects just to complete the tech integration. The 9 global help desks will be cut to 7, and 11 data centers and 22 U.S. corporate business hubs, including the New York headquarters, will be overhauled. "Consolidating systems is an extremely complex, expensive effort," says Dan Stull, managing director at compliance specialist Jefferson Wells Inc. in Seattle.

In Dimon's scheme of things, proprietary technology has a crucial role in boosting future revenues and profits. "Technology improves accuracy, efficiency, and speed, which are the cornerstones to improving client service," says Austin A. Adams, JPMorgan's chief information officer. Nowhere is that clearer than at the retail bank. Each salesperson at a Chase branch is backed by five support people, vs. two at former Bank One branches. Analysts say that JPMorgan also spends $28,300 per employee, more than twice as much as rivals. Apart from saving hundreds of millions, souped-up software will help staff members identify prospects for products. For example, it will highlight people with a bank account but no credit card and vice versa.

POWER MOVE

In an era of acquisitions and mergers, companies need to work hard to maintain brand awareness. Bank One's nearly 2,000 branches are being rebranded with the Chase name.

A makeover of the bank's most conspicuous public face, the retail branches, was long overdue. Chase sat idly by as the rest of the industry underwent a renaissance, sprucing up design, turning tellers into sales associates, and providing come-ons such as free child care and Starbucks coffee. Now, an extra $300 million will fund projects ranging from retraining tellers to rebranding all of Bank One's nearly 2,000 branches with the Chase name starting this spring. Chase will open 175 new branches and hire 1,000 "personal bankers," who, unlike tellers, earn bonuses based on the number of products they sell. Purchases of smaller banks in fast-growing markets such as Florida, New Jersey, and California are also part of the plan, but will be funded separately.

The new troops will have more to sell as Dimon cranks up the bank's $800 billion wealth and asset management businesses. On February 22, Bank One's funds, which were tainted in the mutual-fund scandal, quietly disappeared into a newly retitled JPM Funds, now the nation's fifth-largest fund group, with $200 billion under management. An extra $50 million will bankroll a national ad campaign and 150 new fund

Like many companies aiming to increase profits, JPMorgan is trying to grow by diversifying. It is not only marketing a wider range of products but also going after a wider array of clients.

salespeople. The bank also plans to use its partnership with New York's Highbridge Capital Management—a top-performing $7 billion hedge-fund company in which it bought a controlling interest last September—to create sophisticated investments that aim to generate positive returns even when the stock market is down.

Renewed selling efforts won't be limited to individuals. While other banks and insurance companies are getting out of in-house money management, it is a big growth area for Dimon. Last year the assets that JPMorgan managed for institutions such as U.S. Bancorp and Prudential Financial Inc. were up 80 percent, to $20 billion. The bank is gaining ground in the administration of 401(k) retirement plans, too. Dimon is funneling resources to a 2003 acquisition, Kansas City–based Retirement Plan Services. Last year accounts grew by 40 percent with the addition of clients such as Sun Microsystems and Southwest Airlines. Also, some 30,000 midsize companies on Bank One's client roster will be pitched investment banking and cash-management services that they didn't have before. That alone could bring in $850 million in revenues, because JPMorgan has not only many more relationships with such companies than commercial banks such as BofA but also more capital from which to offer them loans than the likes of Goldman, Sachs & Co. or Lehman Brothers Inc.

Dimon insists that he's not trying to reinvent the classic financial supermarket model that delivers all products to all people. Rather, he is taking rifle shots at those businesses that he believes have the most potential, and he's investing in them even before cost savings are fully in the bag. That's going to make for a rough year for investors, who will have to trust that his vision will work. Loyalists say there's nothing to worry about. They credit Dimon, not Weill, with identifying Citicorp as "the mother of all deals" long before its 1998 merger with Travelers.

"The Sandy mythology is so large it often obscures the contributions that other people made," says Heidi G. Miller, formerly CFO at Citi and now head of JPMorgan's Treasury & Securities Services unit. Either way, Dimon is in no one's shadow at JPMorgan. Success—or failure—will be all his.

CORRECTIONS AND CLARIFICATIONS

"Jamie Dimon's Grand Design" (*Finance*, March 28) should have specified that JPMorgan's international reach was limited in consumer banking; its investment bank operates in 50 countries. Also, while JPMorgan has many dealings with hedge funds, it does not operate a prime brokerage that caters specifically to them. In addition, it ranks third in global M&A, according to Thompson Financial.

POWER MOVE
JPMorgan has been shrewd about capitalizing on the strengths of its partners and its new acquisitions. It is estimated that the bank could rake in $850 million simply by selling services to old Bank One's midsize corporate customers.

UPDATE

Jamie Dimon has grown the total assets of the bank to $1.458 billion from $1.198 billion in 2005. Loans and deposits are up, too. Profits grew from $8.48 million to $14.4 million.

MONDAY MORNING...

THE PROBLEM
Fending off increasingly stiff competition nationally and regionally

Developing businesses that require an infusion of cash at a time when earnings growth is slowing

THE SOLUTION
Sell off portfolios to build a "fortress balance sheet," reserves of cash that can help the company weather hard times.

Track spending closely, requiring units to create their own profit and loss statements and cut out unnecessary expenditures.

Funnel resources into businesses with high potential for growth, hiring more staff, opening up new branches, and updating technology.

Find ways to capitalize on the strengths of partners and new acquisitions.

SUSTAINING THE WIN
Stay focused on the long view and withstand criticism and doubts from investors when the short-term picture looks rocky.

JAMIE DIMON

NORBERT REITHOFER:
BMW'S DREAM FACTORY

POWER PLAYER
Norbert Reithofer's innovations
in management—sharing
the wealth, listening to even
the lowest-ranking workers,
and rewarding risk—have paid
off big time at BMW.

LESSON PLAN

Flatten the management structure, speeding up the decision-making process and enabling the organization to respond to market changes.

Nurture great ideas from every corner of the organization, not just those emanating from the top.

Collaborate across divisions and levels by designing open workspaces that promote formal cross-functional teams.

Make sure that managers set a good example by asking tough questions and listening to people of all ranks, even those who disagree with them.

This 2006 Innovation story was reported by
Gail Edmondson.

49

RISK IS PART OF THE JOB

The car looks like the victim of some mad scientist's experiment gone awry. Inside a research lab in Munich, a BMW 5 Series sedan is splayed open, with electronic gadgets and wires spewing out in all directions. The project: an onboard computer that will recognize you, then seek out the information you want and the entertainment you love. While you sleep, your BMW will scour the Net—via Wi-Fi and other connections—collecting, say, 15 minutes of new jazz followed by a 10-minute podcast on the energy industry. It may sound far-fetched, but for BMW's research wizards, it's yet another way to woo customers by personalizing cars. This intelligent machine will get to know you better every day, constantly learning what you like by monitoring your choices. The brains of the system might even tag along with you on a business trip in the form of a "smart card," instructing the Bimmer you rent in Beijing to load up your daily fix of news and music. When Hans-Joerg Vögel, the 38-year-old project chief, hops in the car's front seat and fires it up, his excitement is palpable. Launching into a riff on the wonders of melding the virtual world with the nuts and bolts of an automobile, Vögel says that the next generation of BMW 5 Series and 7 Series sedans will be the most Net-savvy cars on the road. And if he's right, it'll be because Vögel had the vision to see the importance of the technology and the gumption to build it so that everyone at the automaker could recognize its potential. "We are encouraged to make decisions on our own and defend them," says Vögel. "Risk taking is part of the job."

INNOVATION MACHINE

Vögel's project is only a tiny part of BMW's vast innovation machine. Just about everyone working for the Bavarian automaker—from the factory floor to the design studios to the marketing department—is encouraged to speak out. Ideas bubble up freely, and there is never a penalty for proposing a new way of doing things, no matter how outlandish. BMW, says Ulrich Steger, a professor of management at the

50

International Institute for Management Development in Lausanne, Switzerland, is "a fine-tuned learning system."

TRUE BELIEVERS

That's no small accomplishment, and it has fueled BMW's growth over the past decade from a boutique European automaker to a global leader in premium cars. Although BMW, with $59.2 billion in sales last year, is much smaller than its American rivals, the U.S. auto giants could still learn a thing or two from the Bavarians. Detroit's rigid and bloated bureaucracies are slow to respond to competitive threats and market trends, while BMW's management structure is flat, flexible, entrepreneurial—and fast. That explains why, at the very moment when GM and Ford appear to be in free fall, BMW is more robust than ever. The company has become the industry benchmark for high-performance premium cars, customized production, and savvy brand management, making it the envy of Mercedes-Benz, Audi, and Lexus and the subject of Harvard Business School case studies. Even mighty Toyota Motor Corp. regularly dispatches engineers to BMW's factories to see how the company cranks out 1.3 million customized cars a year.

POWER MOVE

A company that wants fresh thinking should not simply tolerate dissent, but actively encourage it. Rather than letting disagreements fester, BMW workers air their differences openly and work through them. The result: they reach better solutions.

Few companies have been as consistent at producing an ever-changing product line, with near-flawless quality, that consumers crave. BMW has redefined luxury design with its 7 Series, created a mania for its Mini, and maintained some of the widest margins in the industry. A sporty four-wheel-drive coupe and a svelte minivan called the Luxury Sport Cruiser are slated to roll off the production line in 2008. Those models promise to continue BMW's run of cool cars under its new chief executive, Norbert Reithofer, who took over in September.

(His predecessor, Helmut Panke, stepped down upon reaching the mandatory retirement age of 60.) Says Reithofer: "We push change through the organization to ensure its strength. There are always better solutions."

Virtually everyone at BMW is expected to help find those solutions. When demand for the 1 Series compact soared, plant manager Peter Claussen volunteered to temporarily use his brand-new factory—which had been designed for the 3 Series—to crank out 5,000 of the compacts, and he quickly figured out how to do it while maintaining the all-important quality. Last year, line workers in Munich suggested using a smaller diesel engine in the 5 Series, arguing that it would have enough oomph to handle like a Bimmer and be a big seller among those on a tighter budget. They were right. And Panke once insisted that all six members of the management board take an advanced driving course so that they would have a better feel for BMW cars.

POWER MOVE

To encourage employees to develop informal networks, BMW built the Leipzig factory in such a way that no one, including the top echelon, has an enclosed office. All work side by side in open, airy spaces. The only enclosed spaces are small meeting rooms for brainstorming.

Much of BMW's success stems from an entrepreneurial culture that's rare in corporate Germany, where management is usually top-down and the gulf between workers and managers is vast. BMW's 106,000 employees have become a nimble network of true believers, with few hierarchical barriers to hinder innovation. From the moment they set foot inside the company, workers are inculcated with a sense of place, history, and mission. Individuals from all strata of the corporation work elbow to elbow, creating informal networks where they can hatch even the most unorthodox ideas for making better Bimmers or boosting profits. The average BMW buyer may not know it, but when he slides behind the wheel, he is driving a machine born of thousands of impromptu brainstorming sessions. BMW, in fact, might just be the chattiest auto company ever. "The difference at BMW is that [managers] don't think we have all the right answers," says Claussen, manager of the company's new Leipzig factory, a twenty-first-century cathedral of light and air designed by avant-garde architect Zaha M. Hadid. "Our job is to ask the right questions."

It may sound trite, but it sure seems to work. Last year the company sprinted past its stumbling archrival, Mercedes-Benz, in global sales of its BMWs, Minis, and Rolls-Royces. (The German company bought the Rolls name in 1999.) More impressive, BMW's 8.1 percent operating margins make the automaker one of the most profitable in the industry. In the first half of 2006, BMW's sales rose 10.2 percent, to $32 billion, while pretax earnings jumped 44.5 percent, to $3.2 billion, despite a strong euro and punishing increases in raw material costs.

That's not to say that this freewheeling idea factory hasn't made its share of blunders over the years. In 2001, BMW alienated customers with its iDrive control system. The device was designed to help drivers move quickly through hundreds of information and entertainment functions with a single knob, but it proved incomprehensible to many buyers. That misstep could seem minor, though, if BMW were to fail to artfully navigate the challenges ahead. Rival Audi is narrowing the gap with BMW in Europe by churning out a new generation of stylish, high-performance cars that have topped consumer polls. Toyota's Lexus also has BMW in its sights as it makes a move to gain in Europe with sportier, better-handling cars. "We will be challenged—no question," says Reithofer. "We have to take Lexus seriously."

A profit squeeze could just as easily trip up the company in the eyes of investors. To prove he has the right stuff, Reithofer

POWER MOVE

In fast-moving, technology-driven industries, companies need organizational agility to respond swiftly to market changes. Companies like BMW are dealing with the challenge by getting rid of bureaucratic processes, allowing employees to make decisions without many layers of approval.

POWER MOVE

At BMW, humility—and a sense that the company's fate lies in its workers' hands—is ingrained in the culture. New hires learn about 1959, when BMW nearly went bankrupt because it misjudged the market, and how the company recovered through employee innovation.

is going to have to boost margins even as the cost of materials soars. Down the line, the high price of oil and concerns about global warming could make "the ultimate driving machine" a lot less appealing when compared with gas-sipping, eco-friendly cars. The premium market "means extravagance by definition," something that consumers may start to reject, says Garel Rhys, a professor of automotive economics at Cardiff University in Wales.

Yet BMW's greatest danger could be its own growth and success. Says Ralf Kalmbach, a partner at Munich management consultant Roland Berger: "Losing its culture to sheer size is a major risk."

In BMW's favor is an enduring sense that things can go badly wrong. New hires quickly learn that the BMW world as they know it began in 1959. That's when the company nearly went bankrupt and was just a step away from being acquired by Mercedes. That long-ago trauma remains the pivotal moment in BMW folklore. "We never forget 1959," says Reithofer. "It's in our genes, and it drives our performance." If it hadn't been for a bailout by Germany's wealthy Quandt family—still the controlling shareholder, with a 46.6 percent stake—and a pact with labor to keep the company afloat, BMW wouldn't exist today. "Near-death experiences are very healthy for companies," says David Cole, a partner at the Center for Automotive Research in Ann Arbor, Michigan. "BMW has been running scared for years."

The story of 1959 is told and retold at each orientation of new plant workers. Works council chief Manfred Schloch, a 26-year veteran, holds up old, grainy black-and-white photos of two models from the 1950s. The big one was too pricey for a struggling postwar Germany. The other, a tiny two-seater, looked like a toy and was too small to be practical, even by the standards of that era. The company badly misjudged the market, he says. As if handling an ancient, sacred parchment, Schloch pulls out a yellowed, typewritten 1959 plan for turning the company around with a new class of sporty sedans. Schloch then hands out photos of Herbert Quandt and the labor leader of the period, Kurt Golda. "I explain how we rebuilt the company with Quandt's money and the power of the workforce," says Schloch. "And I tell them that's the way it works today, too."

HAPPY WORKERS, BETTER CARS

BMW derives much of its strength from an almost unparalleled labor harmony rooted in that long-ago pact. In 1972, years before the rest of Europe Inc. began to think about pay for performance, the company cut workers in on its profits. It set up a plan that distributes as much as one and a half months' extra pay at the end of the year, provided BMW meets financial targets. In return, the workforce is hyperflexible. When a plant is introducing new technology or needs a volume boost, it's not uncommon for workers from other BMW factories to move into temporary housing far from home for months and put in long hours on the line. Union bosses have made it easy for BMW to adjust output quickly to meet demand. Without paying overtime, the company can crank up production to as much as 140 hours a week or scale it back to as little as 60 hours. The system lets the company provide unprecedented job security, and no one at BMW can remember any layoffs—ever. Since 2000, BMW has hired 12,000 new workers even as General Motors Corp. and Ford Motor Co. have slashed tens of thousands of jobs.

That helps explain why landing a job at BMW is to many Germans what

POWER MOVE

At a time when much of the industry is plagued by labor woes, BMW's relationship with workers is remarkably positive. Employees will work overtime or even relocate temporarily when needed. The reason: BMW pays employees a share of profits and offers job security.

getting into Harvard is for American high school students. The company's human resources department receives more than 200,000 applications annually. Those who make it to an interview undergo elaborate daylong drills in teams that screen out big egos. For the lucky few who are hired, a Darwinian test of survival ensues. BMW promotes talented managers rapidly and provides them with little training along the way, forcing them to reach out to others to learn the ropes. With no one to coach them in a new job, managers are forced to stay humble and work closely with subordinates and with their peers, minimizing traditional corporate turf battles. Anyone who wants to push an innovative new idea learns the key to success fast. "You can go into fighting mode, or you can ask permission and get everyone to support you," says Stefan Krause, BMW's 44-year-old chief financial officer. "If you do it without building ties, you will be blocked."

That BMW's spectacular Leipzig factory was ever built is a testament to the power of such ties. When plant manager Claussen first proposed a competition to lure top architects, headquarters was aghast. "People said to me, 'What's wrong with these guys in Leipzig?'" recalls Krause. "'We don't need beautiful buildings; we need productive buildings.'" But Claussen convinced Krause and others that the unconventional approach would produce not just a pretty factory, but one whose open, airy spaces would improve communication between line workers and managers and create an environment that would help the company build cars better.

Even before Claussen began pushing his architectural vision, others were busy designing the inner workings of the plant. Newly minted engineer Jan Knau was only 27 in 2000 when he was asked to come up with a flexible assembly line for the

POWER MOVE

One way in which BMW promotes a culture of teamwork is by screening out the big egos. New hires undergo rigorous interviews, and young talent is promoted quickly but offered no training so that people are forced to rely on coworkers in order to succeed.

factory. Knau, then just a junior associate, rang up BMW's top 15 assembly engineers, inviting them to a two-day workshop at a BMW retreat near the Austrian Alps. The calls paid off. After a series of marathon sessions that included discussions of every facet of the ideal assembly line, Knau sketched a design with four "fingers," or branches, off the main spine. The branches could be extended to add equipment needed to build new models, making it possible to keep the giant robots along the main line in place rather than moving them for each production change, an expensive and time-consuming process.

Leipzig opened in May 2005, joining Claussen's vision of teamwork enhanced through design to Knau's smart engineering concepts. With pillars of sunlight streaming through soaring glass walls, architect Hadid's design looks more like an art museum than a car factory. Open workspaces cascade over two floors like a waterfall. Unfinished car bodies move along a track, bathed in ethereal blue light, that runs above offices and a smart-looking open cafeteria. If the parade of half-finished cars slows, engineers feel the pulse of the plant change and can quickly investigate the problem. And weekly quality audits—in a plaza that workers pass on their way to lunch—ensure that everyone is quickly aware of any production snafus. The combination of togetherness and openness sparks impromptu encounters among line workers, logistics engineers, and quality experts. "They meet simply because their paths cross naturally," says Knau. "And they say, 'Ah, glad I ran into you, I have an idea.'"

The flexibility of BMW's factories allows for a dizzying choice of variations on basic models. At Leipzig, for instance, parts ranging from dashboards and seats to axles and front ends snake onto overhead conveyer belts to be lowered into the assembly line in a precise sequence

POWER MOVE

BMW pushes all workers to take risks and show initiative. While management sets general objectives, it gives employees the responsibility for figuring out how to reach these objectives and rewards those who do with rapid promotions.

according to customers' orders. BMW buyers can select everything from the engine type to the color of the gearshift box to a seemingly limitless number of interior trims— and then change their mind and order a completely different configuration as little as five days before production begins. Customers love it. They request some 170,000 changes a month in their orders, mostly higher-priced options such as a bigger engine or a more luxurious interior. There are so many choices that line workers assemble exactly the same car only about once every nine months.

That kind of individualization would swamp most automakers with budget-busting complexity. But BMW has emerged as a sort of anti-Toyota. One excels in simplifying automaking. The other excels in mastering complexity and tailoring cars to customers' tastes. That's what differentiates BMW from Lexus and the rest of the premium pack. "BMW drivers never change to other brands," says Yoichi Tomihara, president of Toyota Deutschland, who concedes that Toyota lags behind BMW in the sort of customization that creates emotional appeal.

POWER MOVE

Perhaps the most critical way to ensure that great ideas bubble up is to maintain an open-door policy. The sleek Z4 coupe exists because a young designer's doodle inspired a team to push his concept even though management had already killed the program.

Bottom-up ideas help keep BMW's new models fresh and edgy year after year. Young designers in various company studios from Munich headquarters to DesignWorks in Los Angeles are constantly pitted against one another in heated competitions. Unlike the situation at many car companies, where a design chief dictates a car's outlines to his staff, BMW designers are given only a rough goal and are otherwise free to come up with their best concepts.

To get the most out of its people, BMW likes to throw together designers, engineers, and marketing experts to work intensively on a single project. The redesign of the Rolls-Royce

Phantom, for instance, was dubbed "The Bank" since the 10 team members worked out of an old bank building at London's Marble Arch, where dozens of Rollses roll by daily. "We took designers from California and Munich and put them in a new environment" to immerse them in the Rolls-Royce culture, says Ian Cameron, Rolls's chief designer. The result was the 2003 Phantom, a 19-foot edifice on wheels that remains true to Rolls's DNA, but with twenty-first-century lines and BMW's technological muscle under the hood. With sales of the $350,000 car running at about 700 a year, the Phantom is the best-seller in the superluxury segment, outstripping both the Bentley Arnage and the Mercedes Maybach.

POWER MOVE

Cross-functional teams can be an effective way to solve problems and tap employee knowledge. When designers, engineers, and marketing pros at BMW worked together on the redesign of the Rolls-Royce Phantom, the result was a magnificent blend of twenty-first-century technology and Rolls elegance

Much of BMW's innovation, though, doesn't come via formal programs such as The Bank. In 2001, management decided to pull the plug on the disappointing Z3 sports coupe. But that didn't stop a 33-year-old designer named Sebastian Trübsbach from doodling a sketch of what a Z3 successor might look like. Ulrich Bruhnke, head of BMW's high-performance division, loved it. In Trübsbach's drawing, Bruhnke saw a car that could rival Porsche's Cayman S in performance, but at a lower price. He persuaded a few designers and engineers to carve out some time for the renegade project. Next, Bruhnke gathered a team to map out the business case. The small group toiled for 10 months to build a prototype.

The moment of truth came in November 2004 at a top-secret test track near Munich. Cars were lined up so that the board could examine their styling and proportions in natural light. Only one was covered by a tarp. Panke approached the mystery model. "What is this interesting silhouette?" he asked Bruhnke, who invited his boss to take a look. Panke yanked back the cloth, exposing a glittering, bronze metallic prototype for what would become the Z4 coupe. Bruhnke breathed a sigh of relief when he saw Panke's eyes light up as they swept over the car's curved surfaces. Panke and the board quickly gave the go-ahead, and the Z4 coupe sped to production in just 17 months, hitting showrooms this summer. Bingo. BMW's idea factory wins again.

MONDAY MORNING...

THE PROBLEM
Creating an entrepreneurial culture that rewards bold, risky ideas, while still maintaining organizational discipline and focus

Offering high-quality, customized products to a mass audience

THE SOLUTION
Speed up the transfer of knowledge within the company and break down silos by pushing employees to develop informal networks.

Empower employees to make decisions in the areas in which they have expertise. But be careful to impose cost controls and oversight.

Keep production in an open area so that everyone can see when problems develop.

Encourage employees to be self-starters and flexible by offering financial rewards and job security.

Develop creative ideas by pitting employees against one another in heated competitions in which the best plan wins, no matter where it comes from.

SUSTAINING THE WIN
Keep finding new ways to make a top-notch product better so that the company stays ahead of its competition.

NORBERT REITHOFER

BERNARD ARNAULT:
THE VUITTON MONEY MACHINE

POWER PLAYER
This case study gives an exclusive inside look at the man behind the world's biggest, most profitable luxury brand.

This international cover story, which appeared in 2004, was reported by Carol Matlack, Diane Brady, Robert Berner, Rachel Tiplady, and Hiroko Tashiro.

LESSON PLAN

Maintain the brand's reputation for quality by committing to processes that will ensure that products meet high standards.

Adopt new manufacturing methods that will improve productivity without interfering with quality.

Give the brand an aura of eliteness by spending heavily on glossy ad campaigns and never discounting products.

LEGENDARY TEST LABORATORY

Thunk. Thunk. Thunk. Behind a locked door in the basement of Louis Vuitton's elegant Paris headquarters, a mechanical arm hoists a brown-and-tan handbag a half-meter off the floor—then drops it. The bag, loaded with a $3^{1}/_{2}$-kilogram weight, will be lifted and dropped, over and over again, for four days.

This is Vuitton's test laboratory, a high-tech torture chamber for its fabled luxury goods. Another piece of lab equipment bombards handbags with ultraviolet rays to test their resistance to fading. Still another tests zippers by tugging them open and shutting them 5,000 times. There's even a mechanized mannequin hand, with a Vuitton charm bracelet around its wrist, being shaken vigorously to make sure none of the charms falls off.

Think Louis Vuitton, and what comes to mind? Certainly not a robot that batters bags all day. Most likely, it's those glossy ads—you know, the ones with supermodels draping their lithe frames over Vuitton luggage against a striking gold-and-turquoise desert landscape. Or the crowd of Hollywood celebrities, fashionistas, and even Rudy Giuliani, partying at a champagne-soaked 150th birthday party for Vuitton in a tent next to Lincoln Center in New York last month. Or the sleek new Vuitton retail temples, from Fifth Avenue to Tokyo's fashionable Omotesando district, where shoppers plunk down $1,000 and up for a handbag in the new Murakami line.

Vuitton trades brilliantly in the stuff of desire and ego. Yet creating a buzz is the stock in trade of every fashion and luxury house. Flip through *Vogue*, *Vanity Fair*, or *Elle*, and you'll find pages and pages of half-naked models, legs splayed, dangling handbags from Vuitton and rivals Gucci, Prada, and Hermès. In the glam department, Vuitton is great but not alone.

You have to peek behind the glittery facade to see what makes Vuitton unique—what makes it,

POWER MOVE

Like most high-end brands, Vuitton works hard at cultivating an image of glamour. The company's spends 5 percent of its revenues on fashion advertising, featuring starlets and supermodels.

in fact, the most profitable luxury brand on the planet. There's the relentless focus on quality. (That robot makes sure that Vuitton rarely has to make good on its lifetime repair guarantee.) There's the rigidly controlled distribution network. (No Vuitton bag is ever marked down, ever.) Above all, there's the efficiency of a finely tuned machine, fueled by ever-increasing productivity in design and manufacturing—and, as Vuitton grows ever bigger, the ability to step up advertising and global expansion without denting the bottom line. "Their operating metrics are second to none," says Lew Frankfort, chief executive of U.S. handbag maker Coach, who wants to surpass Vuitton's success someday.

Good luck, Lew. The Vuitton machine is running mighty smoothly right now. With $3.8 billion in annual sales, Vuitton is about twice the size of runners-up Prada and Gucci Group's Gucci division. Vuitton has maintained double-digit sales growth and the industry's fattest operating margins as rivals have staggered through a global downturn the past two years. That power was underscored anew on March 3, when parent LVMH Moët Hennessy Louis Vuitton reported a 30 percent earnings increase for 2003, fueled by a record-high 45 percent operating margin at Vuitton. The average margin in the luxury accessories business is 25 percent. "The sky's the limit," says Yves Carcelle, the charismatic former textile executive who has run Vuitton since 1990 and is widely credited with masterminding its turbocharged growth.

POWER MOVE

To stand out in the crowded luxury market, Vuitton focuses on quality. All products undergo rigorous testing so that the company rarely has to deliver on its lifetime repair guarantee.

LEVITATING ACT

LVMH chairman Bernard Arnault says the brand will keep roaring ahead, even though it has already quintupled sales and increased margins sixfold since he bought the company in 1989: "Of all the luxury brands, Vuitton has the greatest potential for growth." Although LVMH doesn't disclose sales for Vuitton alone, analysts reckon that they grew at least 16 percent worldwide last year and are likely to repeat that feat in 2004. Thanks to Vuitton's levitating act, LVMH's Paris-traded shares have almost doubled in the past 12 months, to more than $75 (60 euros).

Compare that with Gucci, which not only posted disappointing sales and reduced ad spending last year but also was rocked by the announced departure of designer Tom Ford. And whereas Ford had reshaped Gucci in his own rock-star-inspired image, the power of Vuitton extends beyond the persona of well-regarded chief designer Marc Jacobs.

Does Vuitton—which started as a maker of steamer trunks during the reign of Napoleon III—have its best days ahead of it? It still needs to wean itself from Japanese customers, who account for an estimated 55 percent of sales. Vuitton must build sales in the United States while tapping into rising affluence in China and India. It also needs to fight increasingly sophisticated global counterfeiting rings. Most of all, because Vuitton markets itself as an arbiter of style, it needs to keep convincing customers that they're members of an exclusive club.

POWER MOVE

One way in which Vuitton keeps its aura of exclusivity: it never holds sales, and prices continue to rise in the United States and Japan as the euro strengthens.

Carcelle dismisses suggestions that Vuitton has limited growth potential. Yet this is a crucial question for LVMH, which draws an estimated 80 percent of its profits from Vuitton, thus propping up less-successful units, from the DFS duty-free retail chain to couturiers Christian Lacroix and Givenchy. "If LVMH didn't have Louis Vuitton, it would be a disaster," says Armando Branchini of InterCorporate, a Milan luxury consulting group. The touchiness of this issue was underscored recently when LVMH won a ruling in France that a Morgan Stanley analyst, who had cited Vuitton's "maturity," had downgraded LVMH's shares unfairly. Morgan Stanley is appealing the decision, which awarded LVMH at least $39 million in damages.

These are serious concerns. But Vuitton has some serious strengths. One is the loyalty of its clients, shoppers who think one Vuitton bag in the closet just looks too lonely. "I save up for a while, and then I spend a lot on one item," says Elizabeth Hanny, an Indonesian civil servant leaving Vuitton's boutique on Paris's Avenue Montaigne with a cylinder-shaped Papillon monogrammed toile bag that she just bought for $665. Hanny, 35, has shopped at Vuitton since she was 20. Vuitton's strategy is to move such shoppers up from the classic tan-and-brown monogrammed bags to newer lines such as Murakami, which starts at around $1,000, and Suhali, a line of goatskin bags that average more than $2,000.

Women aren't the only Vuitton addicts. Meet Jean-François Bardonnet, 51, an independently wealthy Frenchman who's a sucker for Vuitton briefcases, wallets, even eyeglass cases. "You buy into the dream of Louis Vuitton," he says. "We're part of a sect, and the more they put their prices up, the more we come back. They pull the wool over our eyes, but we love it."

Vuitton was already the world's biggest luxury brand when Arnault acquired it in 1989. But the previous owner, France's Racamier family, had focused mainly on building a Japanese clientele that accounted for 75 percent of sales. Then in the late 1990s, luxury accessories became red-hot, with long waiting lists for bags such as the Kate Spade tote and the Fendi "baguette." Vuitton's classic brown bags, still renowned for their quality, looked dumpy by comparison.

POWER MOVE

As Vuitton learned, freshening up the brand's monogram and introducing new ready-to-wear product lines can help bring in younger consumers.

Enter Jacobs, a streetwise New York designer associated with the grunge look. He seemed a risky choice for Vuitton when Arnault hired him in 1998. But Jacobs's fresh, unfussy aesthetic was a perfect fit, and the new ready-to-wear and shoe lines that he has introduced—though they account for less than 15 percent of Vuitton sales—draw younger customers in the door. Last spring, Jacobs teamed up with Japanese artist Takashi Murakami on a multicolored line of bags, incorporating images like cherry blossoms and eyes into the traditional LV monogram and adding shiny metal trim. Vuitton sold more than $300 million of them last year. "Vuitton is a status symbol, always has been," Jacobs says. "But now it's sexier, bolder." While the Jacobs touch has attracted younger buyers, Vuitton continues to attract older clients with its quality and lifetime free repairs.

Vuitton owes much to Jacobs. But it owes just as much to executives such as Emmanuel Mathieu, a former factory manager at food and beverage giant Danone, who has headed Vuitton's industrial operations since 2000. On Mathieu's watch, Vuitton has boosted manufacturing productivity 5 percent a year, with improvements ranging from more efficient leather-cutting equipment to a new teamwork model in factories loosely modeled on the quality circles pioneered by Japan's automakers. Five years ago, Mathieu says, it took 12 months from the time Vuitton decided to launch a new product until the item hit stores. Now it takes about 6 months. "We're always looking for ways to improve," Mathieu says.

Managers such as Mathieu have helped transform Vuitton from an overgrown cottage industry into a twenty-first-century business. Vuitton's manufacturing is still labor-intensive, with a team of 24 workers producing about 120 handbags a day. But, says Andrew Gowen, a London-based analyst who until recently covered LVMH for Lehman Brothers Inc., "they've achieved pretty close to the perfect balance between mechanization and handmade." Gowen, who has visited the factories of Vuitton and competitor Hermès, says they are "worlds apart. At Hermès, it looks like you stepped into the fourteenth century, just rows and rows of people stitching." Hermès bags cost more, but its operating margins are only about 25 percent.

To see how the Vuitton machine works, consider the Boulogne Multicolor, a new shoulder bag that went on sale this month in Vuitton stores worldwide for about $1,500. With the success of the Murakami line last year, Vuitton marketing executives quickly began looking for a way to capitalize on it. Canvassing store managers, they learned that customers were asking for a Murakami shoulder bag. In a workshop attached to the marketing department, technicians took a classic bag, the Boulogne, reworked it in multicolored toile, added metal studs and other touches, and dubbed it the Boulogne Multicolor. "We wanted to have some elements that were striking, while retaining the history," marketing chief Pascale Le Poivre says. The prototype went directly from the marketing department to top executives, who approved the bag without any involvement of Jacobs's high-profile design team. Moving to production was easy: factories could use existing templates.

TEAMWORK PAYS OFF

By June, the prototype was on its way to Vuitton's factory in Ducey, an airy, glass-sheathed building near the Normandy coast. On the factory floor, workers feed canvas and leather into precision equipment that cuts out the pieces of each bag, cookie-cutter style. Other workers sit at sewing machines, each performing a different task such as stitching in lining.

As at all Vuitton factories, employees at Ducey work in teams of 20 to 30. Each team works on one product at a time, and team members not only are encouraged to suggest improvements in manufacturing but are also briefed on details about the product, such as its retail price and how well it is selling, says Stéphane Fallon, a former manager for Michelin who runs the Ducey factory. "Our goal is to make everyone as multiskilled and autonomous as possible," says team leader Thierry Nogues.

POWER MOVE

Speeding up the manufacturing process can help bring in more profits. Using more efficient leather-cutting equipment and a new teamwork model created by Japanese automakers, Vuitton has drastically cut the amount of time it takes to launch new products.

The teamwork pays off. When the Boulogne Multicolor prototype arrived at Ducey last summer, workers who were asked to make a test production run quickly discovered that the decorative metal studs were causing the zipper to bunch up, adding time and effort to the assembly process. The team alerted factory managers, and within a day or two, technicians had moved the studs a few millimeters away from the zipper. Problem solved.

Such efficiency helps compensate Vuitton for its decision to keep most manufacturing in France, one of the world's most expensive labor markets. Of the 13 factories that make Vuitton bags, 11 are in France—and the other two are across the border in Spain. Why not manufacture someplace cheaper? "The question gets raised all the time, but we feel more confident of quality control in France," says Mathieu.

Productivity alone won't sustain growth. So while most luxury groups cut their ad budgets last year, Vuitton boosted spending an estimated 20 percent, including a global campaign featuring Jennifer Lopez. This year's campaign, shot in the Dubai desert, features supermodels, including Naomi Campbell and Kate Moss. "We used to be modest, too modest," Carcelle says of Vuitton's advertising strategy. "Now we've taken it to a new level." Even so, Vuitton is so big that analysts reckon that it spends only about 5 percent of revenues on advertising, half the industry average.

POWER MOVE

Expanding into emerging overseas markets, like India and China, has helped Vuitton maintain double-digit sales growth and raised the brand's profile. Equally key: it lessened Vuitton's dependence on Japanese customers.

Other companies are trying hard to emulate Vuitton's success. Coach has repositioned its once-utilitarian bag as a snazzy accessory, widening margins to 29 percent. Venerable Hermès is expanding its retail network and recently hired designer Jean Paul Gaultier to freshen its image. Vuitton will try to outpace these rivals as it carefully opens boutiques around the world. Arnault is especially pleased that the U.S.

stores, which once posted 75 percent of their sales to Japanese tourists, now are thronged with local shoppers who account for 85 percent of sales. That's helping Vuitton reduce its risky dependence on Japanese customers. Vuitton's sales in Japan grew 12 percent last year—respectable, but lower than companywide sales growth. "Almost every grown-up Japanese woman already owns at least one Louis Vuitton item," says Akira Miura, chief editor of *WWD Japan*, a fashion paper.

POWER MOVE

Doing business in developing economies can require lots of advance legwork and networking. Before opening stores in India, Vuitton sent a team to meet with a young aristocrat, who, in turn, introduced them to the business and social elite of India.

As Vuitton expands, other hazards are appearing. Counterfeiting has risen sharply in the past five years, largely because of China. Interestingly, Chinese spurn the fake bags, which are mainly exported to Europe and the United States or sold to tourists. Pressed by Vuitton, Chinese authorities closed one factory in Guangzhou last July. "It's a menace we take very seriously," says Bertrand Stalla Bourdillon, director of intellectual property.

Another menace would be the departure of key personnel. Early this year, there was speculation that Jacobs might leave unless LVMH gave more backing to his clothing line. But his contract runs until 2008, and Arnault recently has been singling out Jacobs's label as a rising star in LVMH's portfolio.

For Vuitton, the biggest challenge may be keeping this powerful machine under control. The company opened 18 stores last year, about twice the rate of store openings a decade ago. "The temptation with a lot of brands is to immediately find new outlets, new sources of distribution, and new price points," says Marc Gobé, a New York–based principal in the brand consulting group Desgrippes Gobé. Not Vuitton. "They are extremely disciplined," Gobé says. Arnault promises that Vuitton will never lose its discipline or its focus on quality. "That's what differentiates Louis Vuitton," he says.

The message seems to be getting across. Just ask Ariella Cohen, a 24-year-old Manhattan legal assistant who already owns a Vuitton messenger bag and several Vuitton accessories, and now covets high-heeled Vuitton sandals—even though she'll have to put her name on a waiting list. "Louis Vuitton never goes out of style," she says as she leaves Vuitton's Fifth Avenue store. With luck, the Louis Vuitton machine will never run out of steam.

THE PROBLEM
Increasing sales despite the fact that a large percentage comes from one market

Continuing to attract customers at a time when the company faces intense competition from other luxury brands and cheap knock-offs

THE SOLUTION
Expand into emerging markets overseas. Establish a foothold before rivals do and increase brand awareness globally.

Draw in younger customers by developing new product lines and redesigning the company's monogram.

Push authorities to crack down on counterfeiters, while also maintaining the company's emphasis on quality.

SUSTAINING THE WIN
Keep the company's aggressive expansion efforts without sacrificing the craftsmanship that distinguishes the brand.

BERNARD ARNAULT

HENNING KAGERMANN:
A SEA CHANGE IN SOFTWARE
AT SAP

POWER PLAYER

An inside look at the German legend's move into Lego-like modules provides the keys to revolutionize the way companies do business.

This profile from 2005 was reported by Andy Reinhardt.

LESSON PLAN

Recognize how market forces are reshaping customers' business models. Be willing to radically rethink and alter the kinds of products sold, even at a time of record revenues.

Invest heavily in new technology that will enable the company to fulfill its long-term vision.

Develop a business "ecosystem" by convincing powerhouse companies and other third parties to build goods and services around the company's new products.

Win over new customers by engaging in drastic price cutting, but be prepared for rivals to respond in kind.

NEED FOR SPEED

These are heady days for software giant SAP. The 33-year-old company, based thousands of miles from Silicon Valley in tiny Walldorf, Germany, set the gold standard in the 1990s for software that companies use to manage their businesses. Some 27,000 of the world's largest organizations now automate everything from accounting and manufacturing to customer and supplier relations using SAP software. That makes it far and away the leading seller of big corporate programs, with record revenues last year of $9.5 billion, up 7 percent, and profits of more than $1.6 billion. Analysts predict that revenues will climb 11 percent this year, and SAP shares are near their 52-week highs.

SAP's story sounds rosy except for a nagging problem. Its fiendishly complex and notoriously inflexible programs worked fine for twentieth-century companies. But as a growing number of SAP's customers are embracing a faster, more agile business model, they need software that's simpler and easier to modify. Faced with globalization, outsourcing, changing regulations, and rapid technology shifts, they can't afford to wait for an army of German programmers to release a new software update every few years. "Ten years ago, software customers wanted stability and reliability, and we gave them that," says SAP chief executive Henning Kagermann, 57. "Now they want competitive advantage, differentiation, and, most of all, speed."

POWER MOVE

To thrive in an era of globalization, new technology, and changing regulations, companies need to be adaptive. So SAP changed direction, creating a new generation of software that will enable its customers to modify applications far more easily and inexpensively than before.

Thanks to a dynamic young executive named Shai Agassi, SAP has an answer for that. Ever since SAP acquired Agassi's San Jose (California) start-up, TopTier Software, in 2001, the 36-year-old Israeli has led a campaign inside the company to open up SAP's closed software and make it easier for customers to tweak applications to suit their needs. With Kagermann's strong backing,

Agassi began delivering bits of more flexible software in 2003. Now the scale of Agassi's makeover is becoming clear. Over the next few years, SAP will launch completely revamped products that will be far more malleable than anything the company has offered before.

The move thrusts SAP squarely into the most important—and hotly contested—trend to hit software in a decade. Known as Web services, the new approach uses messages sent over the Net to link up pieces of software running on different computers. Everyone from Microsoft Corp. and IBM to SAP and Oracle Corp. is jumping on Web services because the technology lets customers share information and coordinate work more easily, even linking older systems into state-of-the-art software. "This is going to change the efficiency and productivity of software forever," says Josh Greenbaum, principal of Enterprise Applications Consulting Inc. in Berkeley, California, which advises info-tech vendors and customers.

The migration carries big risks for SAP, though. The software company has already committed an estimated 2,200 software developers and $1 billion in research and development spending to its new technology, which is dubbed NetWeaver. But competitors are developing their own rival programs. SAP's technology won't be fully rolled out until 2007. "SAP has certainly laid out an interesting vision," says Charles Fitzgerald, general manager of platform strategy for Microsoft. "It will be interesting to see how well they deliver on it."

POWER MOVE

Like so many software makers, SAP is striving to speed up its processes. Rather than issuing full-scale software updates once every few years, as it had been doing, SAP now releases improvements piecemeal.

ENGINEERING EDGE

The first pieces of NetWeaver in 2003 were tools to bridge the gap between SAP and non-SAP software. Now SAP has gone much further. It's breaking up its software into smaller chunks that customers can snap together or break apart like Legos.

They're tied together with open Web services. The advantage: customers can pick and choose just the features they need, and even add in chunks provided by companies other than SAP. That will let them create and modify applications faster and more cheaply than they can today.

There's also an engineering benefit for SAP. Its programmers will now be able to develop software in bite-sized pieces, speeding the delivery of new functions. Instead of waiting years between humongous software releases, there can be what the company calls a constant "conveyor belt" of improvements. "This is a game-changer," says Agassi, who joined the SAP executive board in 2002 and was named chief of product development in May.

Industry response to NetWeaver is encouraging. At an SAP convention in May, leading lights of info tech such as Intel, Cisco Systems, EMC, and Adobe pledged to develop products that can work with the software. "SAP is setting the standard that other application vendors will inevitably have to follow," says Nick Earle, Cisco's vice president for Europe, Middle East, and Africa. At the same time, more than 1,300 SAP customers, including Colgate-Palmolive, Aventis, and Whirlpool, are far enough along with NetWeaver that they're willing to serve as references for potential buyers.

So far NetWeaver hasn't contributed to SAP's revenues. Most of it is now bundled for free into other SAP software. But if NetWeaver catches on, SAP has an opportunity to gain enormous power and influence. Like Microsoft Windows on desktop PCs and servers, NetWeaver could define an industry standard for creating new business applications. Thousands of independent developers could start writing specialized programs that plug into the NetWeaver framework. That would give SAP entrée to millions of new customers whose businesses were too small or whose needs were

POWER MOVE

One way to build a thriving business "ecosystem" around a new product is to line up big-name supporters. SAP convinced Microsoft, Intel, Cisco Systems, and Adobe to deliver products that would accommodate SAP's new software approach.

too esoteric to use SAP's older, one-size-fits-all packages, which could cost hundreds of millions of dollars and also take years to install.

To build a new ecosystem around NetWeaver, SAP is turning on the charm. Six months ago it hired George Paolini, the executive who marketed the wildly popular Java programming language for Sun Microsystems Inc., to lure outside developers. Some 132,000 have already signed up for an

online network that provides information and technical help. SAP also has managed to attract more than 200 top managers from Oracle, BEA Systems, and Siebel Systems in the past 18 months.

Still, many questions remain about NetWeaver. For one, SAP hasn't yet disclosed pricing for the modular version of its software. The danger is that customers could buy less software from SAP or use more products from other vendors. Kagermann doesn't seem worried. By helping SAP customers "become more flexible and competitive," NetWeaver will help keep them in the SAP fold, he says.

Then there's the competitive threat. Both Microsoft and IBM do far more business in partnership with SAP than in competition. But each has its own approach to Web services that differs from SAP's. Over time, that could become a source of friction. "They're trying to build a world where everything is built around SAP applications. I just don't think it's going to work," says Mark Hanny, vice president for alliances at IBM Software Group. "It's a heterogeneous world. This is very limiting."

TRENCH WARFARE
Oracle is a more direct worry. It has announced a project called Fusion that will unite its own software with the disparate product lines it acquired last year from California-based PeopleSoft, a major provider of business applications, and then

link up the pieces with Web services. Oracle executives say that their approach will be more open than NetWeaver. "SAP's products are built using proprietary language that is decades old," says Oracle CEO Lawrence J. Ellison. "Fusion applications are built entirely on industry standards." The PeopleSoft merger is already paying off: On June 29, Oracle said combined application license sales grew 52 percent in the fourth quarter. Still, SAP has a healthy head start. The first parts of Oracle's ambitious revamping are promised for 2008, a whole year after SAP's project is set to be finished.

Long before either company completes its makeover, each is fighting trench warfare to grab customers today. In January, SAP began offering Oracle customers credits worth up to 75 percent of the value of their software if they switch to SAP. It claims that 10 have done so since the PeopleSoft acquisition, including Samsonite, which announced its move on June 21. Oracle recently announced a retaliatory offer giving SAP customers 100 percent credit on their old software if they change to Oracle. It claims to have nabbed a half-dozen SAP customers in recent months. Still, Goldman Sachs projects that SAP's market share among the top four corporate applications sellers will climb from 62 percent at the end of 2004 to 72 percent this year, while Oracle's falls from 28 percent to 19 percent.

POWER MOVE

Slashing prices is a reliable, if risky, way to lure customers away from rivals. SAP has offered credits of up to 75 percent to Oracle customers who switch to SAP packages, but Oracle has responded with 100 percent credits to customers who switch from SAP.

SAP users are starting to tell stories about NetWeaver that lend credibility to the company's strategy. London-based Rexam PLC, the world's leading aluminum can producer and number five in packaging overall, is using NetWeaver to radically overhaul its manufacturing. Rexam used to keep on hand a hoard of five-ton aluminum coils used for making cans. Now, by using SAP's software to link suppliers directly into its manufacturing, Rexam has suppliers keep track of its inventory via the Net and automatically send replacements as coils are used up. That has let Rexam cut on-hand supply of its most expensive component by half. What's more, says chief information officer Paul Martin, "suppliers like it, too, because it helps them manage their own businesses better."

Users such as Rexam could go even further now that SAP is releasing more pieces of NetWeaver. In May, the company published a catalog of 500 SAP software objects, each of which performs a defined business process such as the book-to-bill sequence. Customers or consultants can use these objects to build new software applications.

The success of SAP's long-term vision lies in attracting an army of independent software developers to support NetWeaver. Some 150 third-party programs that have been built for NetWeaver are already available, Paolini says, and analysts figure that the number could top 500 by 2006. That should help SAP burrow into potentially thousands of niche markets that are too small for it to pursue on its own. Modular software also could help SAP dive deeper into small and midsize businesses, the fastest-growing segment of the market, where it faces growing competition from giant Microsoft.

POWER MOVE

Hiring key executives away from competitors can help give a firm a head start in a new market. SAP hired George Paolini, who marketed Java for Sun Microsystems, to lead SAP's push to get programmers writing software that works with SAP's.

A decade ago, SAP improved the way businesses operate. Now the company wants to change the entire software industry. "We could have sat back and waited for the storm to pass, but it never will," says Agassi. "Instead, we decided to lead it." Ambitious, yes, but in high tech nobody ever got ahead by holding back.

MONDAY MORNING...

THE PROBLEM
Reinventing the company's wildly successful strategy as corporate customers' needs evolve because of large-scale economic changes

Staying ahead in a field that is filled with aggressive, top-notch competitors

THE SOLUTION
Create cutting-edge products that will give clients what they desire most: speed and flexibility.

Build an army of supporters by convincing software developers and other third parties to create programs around the firm's new products.

Staff the company with experienced pros from rival firms, who will have the know-how and credibility to implement the new vision.

SUSTAINING THE WIN
Keep thriving by continuing to look beyond the present, forecasting industry changes and refining strategy accordingly.

HENNING
KAGERMANN

ROGER K. DEROMEDI: WHY KRAFT IS ON A CRASH DIET

POWER PLAYER
This mini-case study looks at Roger Deromedi's plan to bolster Kraft's sagging brands. In 2006, Irene Rosenfeld took over as CEO, replacing Deromedi.

Divest the company's sluggish-selling secondary brands, and concentrate instead on shoring up its core businesses.

Increase sales by developing products that are truly new and inventive, not simply rehashes of old ones.

LESSON PLAN

This news analysis and commentary was reported by Michael Arndt in 2004.

SLIM DOWN TO GROW

Kraft Foods Inc. sure has bulked up. In the past five years, the company has gobbled up 10 rivals, including Nabisco Holdings Corp. for $19 billion in late 2000. The result: the biggest packaged-food maker in the United States, with expected 2004 sales of $32.3 billion and products in almost every aisle of the grocery store, from Kraft cheeses and Oreo cookies to Oscar Mayer meats, Post cereals, DiGiorno pizzas, and Maxwell House coffees.

Now chief executive Roger K. Deromedi has decided that it's time for Kraft to slim down. He began with the November 15 sale of Kraft's Life Savers and Altoids candies to Wm. Wrigley Jr. Co. for $1.5 billion in cash. And more will follow, he says, as Kraft divests itself of other laggard and peripheral product lines to concentrate on the blockbuster brands that can be tops in their categories worldwide. Says Deromedi: "We want the products that consumers and retailers are more excited about."

POWER MOVE With the retail sector increasingly being dominated by giants like Wal-Mart, consumer-goods companies have lost leverage and are under pressure to give retailers what they want. And what retailers want are the top sellers

Clearly, the pressure is on the 51-year-old Deromedi, who became Kraft's sole CEO a year ago, when co-chief executive Betsy Holden was demoted to global marketing president. Like other consumer-goods companies, Kraft is scrambling to give Wal-Mart Stores Inc. and other retailing giants what they want. Bulking up to gain leverage with the retail behemoths fueled much of Kraft's expansion in the first place, but that strategy hasn't worked. With Wal-Mart and others increasingly being interested only in the briskest-selling products, it turns out that suppliers are better off with a clutch of category killers than with a cartful of so-so sellers.

But dealing with Wal-Mart isn't Kraft's only problem. Many of its problems are of its own making, from turmoil within its executive suite to oversaturating store shelves with too many variations of the same old product. How many different kinds of Oreos do consumers really want? At the same time, other consumer-products companies, notably Procter & Gamble Co., have been far more skillful in navigating the retailing shoals with nifty new products. What's more, management at Kraft's parent, Altria Group Inc., is putting the squeeze on Kraft to shape up in advance of a possible spin-off of its controlling stake next year.

POWER MOVE

In an intensely competitive industry, companies can see their laggards and ancillary holdings as expensive distractions. Kraft is dumping its slow-selling and secondary brands so that it can focus on building the brands that have the potential to be best-sellers.

CARB LOADS

While investors generally endorse Deromedi's new focus, trimming the weakest links alone won't be enough. He will also need to bolster sales and margins for the brands he keeps to lift Kraft from a profit slump that goes back to 2003. That won't be easy. Private-label brands are undermining Kraft's ability to charge premium prices, and the consolidating retail sector leaves Kraft with fewer outlets. At the same time, many of its staples, such as Nabisco cookies and crackers, are verboten under low-carb diets, while its own low-carb alternatives haven't scored.

POWER MOVE

At a time when the marketplace is inundating consumers with endless choices, selling yet another variation on Oreos won't give a company a competitive advantage. The companies that are thriving are offering new, groundbreaking products.

But Deromedi says the asset sales will help. Already, the Northfield (Illinois)–based company has bumped up its 2004 marketing budget by some $550 million, swelling outlays on marketing, administration, and R&D to more than $6.5 billion. And as Kraft raises more money, Deromedi promises to further boost spending on ads and product development, such as its new DiGiorno microwavable pizzas. Says Deromedi: "Where we think we can win is the key."

POWER MOVE

Even blockbuster products can experience drops in sales as consumer trends change. Kraft found, for instance, that when low-carb diets took off, sales of its cookies and crackers went down.

Now Deromedi is evaluating which brands to auction off next. As with the sale of Altoids and Life Savers to Wrigley, he'll look at secondary brands or those where Kraft lacks the clout with retailers to turn things around. Analysts and consultants figure Oscar Mayer is most likely. Despite being the leader in bacon, hot dogs, and luncheon meats in the United States, with $2.1 billion in annual sales, it has been losing out to cheaper store brands and has little brand recognition overseas. Kraft's $1.2 billion-a-year Post cereals division, a distant number three that also is ceding market share, could also be on the block. Michael A. Crowe, a senior managing director of Mesirow Financial, which owns 200,000 Kraft shares, hopes the sales come soon. "It's not long overdue," he says. "But it is overdue."

Long-term, of course, Deromedi cannot make Kraft grow by slimming down. In fact, he says he might take some of the proceeds from divestitures and make acquisitions. But for now, it seems, Kraft may do well to drop a few more pounds.

MONDAY MORNING...

THE PROBLEM
Turning around a large conglomerate that has been beset by declining profits and sales and that faces tough competition from store brands

THE SOLUTION
Raise cash by dumping the company's weakest brands, and pump that money into new product development and marketing.

Gain traction with retail chains by offering fewer—and more popular—products for sale.

SUSTAINING THE WIN
Track consumer tastes closely and move quickly to capitalize on new trends.

ROGER K.
DEROMEDI

STEVE STOUTE:
REPOSITIONING ANY BRAND
WITH POP CULTURE

POWER PLAYER
Steve Stoute is making hot sellers out of cold brands by turning executives on to "the tanning of America"—he calls his firm "a McKinsey of pop culture."

LESSON PLAN

Recognize that rap and hip-hop culture is not simply a subculture, but is shaping a new generation of consumers.

Create a bond with young customers by adopting their language, music, and icons and incorporating them into ads.

Tap the knowledge of young employees and turn them into evangelists for the brand.

This 2007 story was reported by Tom Lowry.

HIP-HOP AND PRACTICALITY

Several months into his new job as vice president of U.S. marketing and advertising for General Motors, Mike Jackson came to the conclusion that the automaker was just not cool enough. Young, urban trendsetters on the East and West Coasts were not paying attention to GM's cars. The message being sent to consumers, Jackson says, was all wrong. "We worried far too much about the sheet metal, color, etc.," he explains. "What we really needed to worry about was connecting emotionally with our consumers." So Jackson picked up the phone last spring and called Steve Stoute.

Other executives who are overseeing brands that have gone stale are also turning to the 36-year-old consultant and former music executive for help. Stoute's agency, Translation Consultation & Brand Imaging, offers to imbue brands with a combination of hip-hop ethos and practicality to help reposition products, from Chevy Impalas to Crest Whitestrips to Reese's peanut butter cups. The end result is for brands to resonate with a younger, more trendy audience. Other successful entrepreneurs have emerged from the hip-hop scene, such as Russell Simmons and Sean "P. Diddy" Combs, to help put urban fashion and lifestyle into the mainstream. But Stoute is more closely aligned with a new guard of innovation consultants providing strategies that go beyond tricked-out sneakers and jeans. His message: companies have not embraced the changes in the culture to be able to talk to a new generation of consumers. "So many executives," says Stoute, "are lost in the confines of their own building." Besides GM, Stoute has successfully taken his mantra to clients that include McDonald's, Procter & Gamble, Hershey, Microsoft, and Estée Lauder.

POWER MOVE

Young consumers—white, black, and Latino—have had their tastes, values, and experiences shaped by rap and hip-hop culture. So to reach the youth culture, brands have to adopt its lingo and signposts. McDonald's, for instance, created its "I'm lovin' it" campaign using Justin Timberlake.

Now Stoute seems to be gaining respect on Madison Avenue. Interpublic Group of Companies Inc., the $6.2 billion-a-year global advertising conglomerate, is in talks with Stoute to buy a majority stake in Translation, say sources close to those talks. If the deal is closed, IPG would get schooled on Stoute's approach to brands and access to celebrities, while Translation would gain entrée to IPG's large client base and deeper pockets.

POWER MOVE

When young employees believe in a brand, they can be powerful emissaries for it. For instance, Stoute suggested that McDonald's redesign its workers' uniforms so that they were cool enough that employees would proudly wear them on days off.

As an African American with strong relationships with hip-hop artists (music icon Jay-Z is a good friend and business partner), Stoute knows how easy it is to pigeonhole Translation as a black ad agency. He immodestly characterizes his firm as "a McKinsey of pop culture." By that he means that Translation is called upon by companies that are facing strategic challenges. "These are companies that know they have to take advantage of global trends, but at the same time are afraid of jeopardizing core businesses," says Stoute. "We show them how to walk that thin line. It often comes down to showing them the language and tonality needed to reach consumers."

But Stoute also says he's helping executives understand a phenomenon that he refers to as the "tanning of America." It's a generation of black, Latino, and white consumers who have the same "mental complexion," he says, based on "shared experiences and values." Rap and hip-hop, starting in the late 1980s when white suburban kids began snapping up music by mostly inner-city artists, provided the first glimpse into this shift. "Rap was a litmus test for where the culture was headed," he says.

To connect McDonald's to this world, Stoute helped create its "I'm lovin' it" ad campaign featuring pop star Justin Timberlake. That was relatively easy. To top executives, it was all about coming up with a new ad. Stoute has encouraged them to go much further and told them they could be blowing a big opportunity for reaching young adults. They have a million-plus young people working for them who come to the job every day ashamed of what they're wearing. "The uniforms are ugly," says Stoute. "If the workers were actually proud of what they were wearing, it could be a huge opportunity to promote the brand. Those kids wouldn't want to change after work and stuff it in a knapsack."

Stoute suggested that McDonald's hire top designers to redo the uniforms under urban-centric brands such as Sean John, Rocawear, FUBU, American Apparel, and Tommy Hilfiger. The chain is considering the move. "We know the cutting edge comes from the African American and Hispanic communities," says Bill Lamar, McDonald's senior vice president of marketing, "but then crosses all people."

POWER MOVE

If you want your brand to feel contemporary, you have to get out of your office and off the golf course. To keep in touch with youth culture, Stoute will visit stores and malls to eavesdrop and watch how people shop.

Stoute knows those communities well. Raised in Queens, New York, he was barely out of his teens when he became a road manager for the rap act Kid 'n Play. He would go on to become a manager for rapper Nas and a young female hip-hop soul singer named Mary J. Blige, now one of the music industry's biggest successes, who won three Grammy Awards this year. From there, Stoute was recruited by Sony Music and later Interscope Records of the Universal Music Group. But he was becoming fascinated with the broader playing field of brands. He left music to join veteran ad man Peter Arnell as a partner in his business, the Arnell Group. At Arnell in 2003, Stoute worked with Reebok, at the time a stagnant brand that needed to revamp its image. He brokered Reebok's ad campaign with Jay-Z, whose S. Carter Collection by Rbk (Jay-Z's real name is Shawn Carter) made Reebok a big hit on city streets. "Steve was very good at getting our whole organization to buy in on this new direction," says former Reebok CEO Paul Fireman, who worked closely with Stoute to revive the brand. There was resistance from the organization. "Sometimes the fear factor rose quickly," says Fireman. "But he made a very strong case for why we needed to be more cosmopolitan." The breakthrough for Stoute was convincing Reebok's executives that you couldn't position the sneakers on performance capabilities. "Nike had that locked up," says Stoute. "Instead, they needed to align the brand to the sound and rhythm of sports, with fashion."

"RETAIL THEATER"
Following the sale of the Arnell Group to ad giant Omnicom, Stoute launched Translation in 2004 with a 10 percent investment from his old employer, Interscope Records. Now housed in the penthouse of a 12-story midtown Manhattan building, Translation employs nearly 50 people. Stoute has his own method for keeping in touch with contemporary culture. He frequently invites his cohorts to join him for what he calls "retail theater." He loves going to department stores and malls to watch people. "I like to see how they touch fabric or view a display," he says. "Or listen to what they say to their husbands. For me, it is more fun than going to the movies."

Stoute works most closely with two top deputies. Charles Wright, Translation's chief strategy officer, spent seven years in marketing and product management at major record labels, including Motown and Virgin. Stoute's other deputy is vice president for strategy John McBride, an industrial designer by training who last worked as a research scientist and project director in Eastman Kodak's innovation hub.

Once a client hires them, Stoute, Wright, and McBride often brainstorm ideas early on with sketches, music, and video clips. When Hewlett-Packard Co. came calling three years ago, the challenge was to create HP brand awareness in the home entertainment area. Compared with slick products from Apple and Sony, says McBride, HP wasn't regarded as a real player, making it hard for the PC maker to claim, "We're cool, too." So Translation started by signing Gwen Stefani to sing her hit *Hollaback Girl* to help promote digital cameras. Most recently, during HP's "The Computer Is Personal Again" campaign, Stoute once again called on Jay-Z, who helped launch ads in which the rapper is heard but his face is never seen. That helped give HP celebrity appeal, says McBride.

Still, not all of Stoute's ideas fly. Some companies view them as just too far out. When Stoute tried to help Coors overhaul its brand, he suggested less emphasis on the brand's "rugged" image and its brewing processes and more effort to create a new high-end aura. Says Stoute: "We were attempting to make Coors an arbiter in the renaissance of sophisticated beer drinking." The pitch didn't make it.

But Stoute's most important test will be changing perceptions about GM. The assignment is to help increase awareness of the carmaker's models among a growing and influential buyer group, 18- to 34-year-olds who live in clustered metropolitan areas on the coasts and along the perimeter of the southern United States. The task is to get them to think about GM the way they were already thinking about Toyota and other Japanese models. The mandate, says Stoute, was "to think of ways to spark contagious consumer behavior."

POWER MOVE

A tried-and-true way to create buzz is to stage a big, splashy event. GM threw a glitzy fashion show featuring cars and young celebrities, hoping that it would help change the company's image

So far, Translation has helped GM to redeploy Tiger Woods from the Buick brand to what Stoute believes is a more convincing role, as a spokesman for all of GM. "Tiger and GM share similar values of integrity and, most importantly, diversity," he says. Stoute also connected GM with Jay-Z on Jay-Z Blue, a branded, lavender-tinted, electric blue that will be available on the GMC Yukon. Translation is also creating a campaign for the reissue of the Camaro, the iconic 1970s muscle car. Stoute is talking with the advertising agencies responsible for all GM models about marketing alternatives, such as social media, that go beyond traditional TV and print outlets.

It's still too early to tell if GM is reaching new consumers. Unsurprisingly, Stoute believes the results so far are positive. Look no further, he says, than the January debut of Jay-Z Blue. From Detroit to Beijing, the news was featured on the front pages of 26 national and international Sunday papers.

On the night of the premiere of Jay-Z Blue, Stoute was in Detroit backstage in a green room. He had flown in from New York with Jay-Z to introduce the color and help kick off a GM-sponsored fashion show of cars and celebrities, the first of its kind for the automaker. As Stoute sipped a Budweiser in a large, heated tent erected for the event not far from GM's headquarters, he mingled with supermodel Petra Nemcova, actor Christian Slater, and Oscar winner Jennifer Hudson. Not far from the spread of catered food were surfing star Laird Hamilton and model and actress Carmen Electra. GM's marketing chief Jackson gushed that the glamorous scene had just the kind of glitzy excitement he had hoped would envelop GM when he hired Stoute.

FEELING CHEVY

Since that big night, Stoute has focused most intently on the stodgy Chevrolet brand. The challenge was to make Chevys more appealing to those with "a metro mindset, that 34-year-old independent-thinking person," says Ed Peper, general manager of Chevrolet. "One of the first things Steve asked us was: do you know that there have been 700 songs written about Chevy? Why aren't you leveraging that?'" It became abundantly clear to Peper that Chevy hadn't done enough to marry its brand with music. So Stoute suggested bringing in Grammy-winning hip-hopper T.I. to help sell the Impala. An ad campaign featuring T.I.'s song *Top Back* first aired on MTV and Black Entertainment Television in early February.

Chevy, in turn, sponsored T.I.'s latest music video. T.I. appears in another spot that GM is calling "Ain't We Got Love," which was launched during the Super Bowl. The spot also features Mary J. Blige, Dale Earnhardt Jr., and a group of regular folks fawning over their cars. "It's damn near an emotion driving a Chevy," says Stoute. "We want people to feel that."

MONDAY MORNING...

THE PROBLEM
Making a brand "cool" and popular among young, urban trendsetters

THE SOLUTION
Keep abreast of contemporary culture. Don't just read studies—go into the field and observe what people buy and what they say about and do with products.

Make a brand hip by promoting it with edgy music and performers.

Listen to young consumers, especially those at your company. If your young workers don't believe in your brand, you'll face an uphill battle getting consumers to believe in it. Young employees also can help you understand the brand's strengths and weaknesses.

SUSTAINING THE WIN
To continue to reach young consumers, think expansively and creatively about promotion, moving beyond traditional TV and print ads into social media.

STEVE STOUTE

97

TRENDS

SPEED DEMONS

Smart companies are creating new products—and whole new businesses—almost overnight by partnering with other companies and with outsourcers. New ideas are generated by tapping outsiders and organizing off-site sessions for employees. Workflows are being reassessed to identify the unwritten rules that slow down or prevent innovation. Companies are developing an appetite for risk, recognizing that you have to fail once in a while in order to produce a steady stream of hits.

SPEED, THE ULTIMATE WEAPON
Last year on February 14, 2005 Virgin Group Ltd. founder Sir Richard Branson got a provocative e-mail out of the blue.

Gotham Chopra, son of self-help guru Deepak Chopra, had a proposal: Branson should team up with Indian entrepreneurs who were running a comics distribution business and create a new global comics and animation powerhouse—part Marvel Comics, part Pixar. It fit Virgin's brand: Kids. Fun. Big. Risky. Branson asked his people to check it out. Boom! Bang! Shazam! By July it looked like a done deal, except for one thing. Virgin was moving so fast that none of its executives had ever laid eyes on the operation that was meant to be the heart of its new venture. "I needed to go to India to make sure it wasn't a shack in the jungle," says Virgin Books Ltd. chief Adrian Sington.

It wasn't, and Virgin Comics LLC was born. The company was revealed to the world on January 6, and now Branson and Virgin Comics Chief Executive Sharad Devarajan are sketching out grand plans. They hope to build India into a multibillion-dollar comics market by plying its under-20 population of 500 million with mythic tales. And there may be huge opportunities for export to the West. Seven titles are due out in the United States, Britain, and India in the coming months. Even animated movies and TV shows are on the drawing boards in Bangalore.

Virgin's quick entry into comics spotlights one of the most intriguing shifts in business today. Speed is emerging as the ultimate competitive weapon. Some of the world's most successful companies are proving to be expert at spotting new opportunities, marshaling their forces, and bringing new products or services to market in a flash. That goes for launching whole new ventures, too.

Virgin, which made its name in music, megastores, and airlines, may be the exemplar. In short order, it has entered one new business after another, including mobile phones, credit cards, bikes, fitness clubs, books, hotels, games, trains, consumer electronics, even space travel. "A good idea for a new business tends not to occur in isolation, and often the window of opportunity is very small," explains Branson. "So speed is of the essence."

The pace is picking up across such industries as retailing, consumer goods, software, electronics, autos, and medical devices. In many realms, the time it takes to bring a product to market has been cut in half during the past three or four years. At Nissan Motor Co., the development of new cars used to take 21 months. Now, the company is shifting to a $10^1/2$-month process. In the cell phone business, Nokia, Motorola, and others used to take 12 to 18 months to develop basic models. Today, they take six to nine months.

It's all being driven by a new innovation imperative. Competition is more intense than ever because of the rise of the Asian powerhouses and the spread of disruptive new Internet technologies and business models. Companies realize that all of their attention to efficiency in the past half-decade was fine—but it's not nearly enough. If they are to thrive in this hypercompetitive environment, they must innovate more and faster.

Of course, speed has been important in business ever since the California Gold Rush. What's changed in recent years is that a slew of new techniques make it possible to get things done much faster. Start with global outsourcing. A vast network of suppliers around the world stands ready to do everything from manufacturing products to drawing up legal contracts. This helps companies create supply chains that are faster, more flexible, and more efficient than ever before.

POWER PLAY

In a hypercompetitive economy, the companies that succeed are those that are willing to experiment—and stumble occasionally. A flop isn't necessarily a sign of weakness. In fact, it can be viewed as evidence of inventiveness—as long as the firm also has plenty of wins.

AT THEIR FINGERTIPS
Take clothing retailer H&M. Every time it designs a new outfit, the Swedish company can choose on the fly among more than 700 manufacturers worldwide. It looks for the right skills, geographic proximity, and ability to finish the job quickly— and then gets the plant rolling in a matter of hours or days. Or consider Wipro Ltd., the Indian outsourcing firm. It does engineering and design for clients, and in some cases, part of its

fee is based on the success of the product it delivers. Customers can keep costs low until they know they've got a hit on their hands. "Our clients are under a lot of pressure to get new products faster into the market. Their core employment isn't adequate for it, so they're looking for partners who can do it for them," says Azim Premji, Wipro's chairman.

Then there's technology. The Internet has become ubiquitous, so companies can connect with talent anywhere in the blink of an eye, inside or outside the company. Open-source software can be plucked off the shelf to become the foundation of new software programs or Web sites. Algorithms can be used to slice and dice market information and spot new trends.

Perhaps most important, today's fleet companies are embracing a management approach that would have been heresy just a decade ago: if you don't fail occasionally, you're not pushing hard enough. Executives tend to try lots of things, expecting a number of them to flop. It doesn't matter as long as you produce a steady stream of hits. Even losers can burnish a company's reputation for innovation if they're seen as exciting experiments. "It's not just O.K. to fail; it's imperative to fail," says Seth Godin, a marketing expert and author of several books, including *Unleashing the Ideavirus*.

Virgin has had its share of flops. One example: it formed Virgin Electronics in July 2004 and sold only a modest number of digital music players through that holiday season. Branson, who gets out as fast as he gets in, shut down the business in March 2005. Google Inc. may be the highest-profile example of the new philosophy. It launches product after product, more than 100 in the past five years. Not all of them soar; one that didn't was Froogle, the comparison-shopping site. Marissa Mayer, who helps guide the company's innovations, says Google wants to try new things and see what resonates with its users. This approach, says Mayer, "frees you from fear."

In this world of possibility, laggards end up losers. The most aggressive companies tap into outsourcers for new products or use the Net to pull in ideas from unknown geniuses in Bangalore or Beijing. Rivals must follow suit or fall behind. The cell phone business is just one sector where the competition is more intense than ever. Motorola came out a year ago with the RAZR, its ultrathin cell phone with camera and music player. Samsung Group answered with the Blade seven months later. Then on February 1, Motorola came back with its SLVR, a phone that's even more svelte than its predecessor. "It's like having a popular nightclub. You have to keep opening new ones. To stay cool, you have to speed up," says Michael Greeson, president of market researcher Diffusion Group Inc.

POWER PLAY

Traditional clothing retailers typically design items at least six months ahead of time. But H&M, the Stockholm-based fashion retailer, is able to ship clothes into stores in as little as three weeks. Its secret: the organization is flat. The people in charge of each collection track trends closely and have the power to move on new ideas quickly.

A higher tolerance for failure doesn't mean ignoring the risks, of course. In certain sectors, a string of losers can spell trouble. While consumer-electronics companies pump out new products at a frantic pace, the industry as a whole barely ekes out a profit. "If you're not fast, you're dead. But if you're not also good, you're still dead," says George Bailey, a consultant at IBM Business Consulting Services.

Opting out is not an option, though. To goose revenues and profits, companies must introduce more products and jump into new markets. There are probably as many good recipes for up-tempo innovation as there are successful companies. No one model works for all industries, or even all companies within a single sector. Yet when *BusinessWeek* pinged dozens of companies to see how they do things fast, patterns emerged. Here are some of their best practices for making the journey from concept to market.

POWER PLAY

As 37signals, a Chicago software firm, has learned, being bigger doesn't necessarily mean being better. Great ideas can get stuck in bottlenecks in large, bureaucratic organizations. Thus, 37signals deliberately keeps its staff small because this enables the firm to respond quickly to market changes. Large companies, like restaurant franchiser Raving Brands, can get new concepts going with small teams.

FIND NEW WAYS TO SPOT HITS

While focus groups and market research are useful, they're not sufficient. So companies have come up with new techniques for sussing out great ideas. Electronics retailer Best Buy Co. has begun checking with venture capitalists to find out what their start-ups are working on. Procter & Gamble Co. uses online networks to get in touch with thousands of experts worldwide. That helped the company produce 100 new products in the past two years. One example: it found a professor in Bologna, Italy, who had invented an inkjet method for printing edible images on cakes. P&G used it to create Pringles potato chips with jokes and pictures printed on them— boosting Pringles growth into double digits. "This was terrific. We found a ready-to-go solution we could put into the marketplace," says Larry Huston, P&G's vice president for research and development. The product came out in one year, rather than the usual three or four.

KEEP YOUR LAUNCH TEAM AGILE

Everybody knows that bureaucracy means death to new ideas, yet most companies still insist on forcing innovative products and ventures through a gauntlet of presentations and reviews and refinements. Not at Raving Brands, an Atlanta-based fast-casual restaurant franchiser. Chief executive Martin Sprock talks a mile a minute and launches concepts nearly as fast. In the past five years, Sprock has unveiled six, including Fresh Mex, Asian fusion, and gourmet salads, and has another on the way. Raving Brands typically goes from finished concept to store opening in about a year. For some franchisers, it takes two years or more.

Raving Brands isn't so much a company as a SWAT team in chinos and polo shirts. Sprock meets with four or five senior partners every Monday to handle problems and talk over new ideas. There isn't a corporate office, so they gather at one of the restaurants. Sprock might come in with a new concept. (The gourmet salad idea came after he saw fancy salads being custom-made for busy New York office workers.) They'll bat around ideas. Then they'll split up to handle their specialties—recipes, say, or real estate. If somebody needs a quick O.K., they get Sprock on his cell. "We take a lot of pride in moving quickly and not having a committee sitting around and planning things," he says.

BREAK YOUR UNWRITTEN RULES

Every company has them. They're those mental crutches that say this is the way we do it because this is the way we've always done it. For routine matters, that's fine. But not when you're trying to create something new, and quickly. There's probably no industry more staid than wine. California's Jackson Enterprises was no exception, until it had to scramble to deal with a huge worldwide glut of wine in late 2004. Rather than pour juice down the drain, the company, known for its Kendall-Jackson brand, decided to do nearly everything differently. "We absolutely broke all the unspoken rules," says Laura Kirk Lee, the marketer who led this campaign.

POWER PLAY

These days, focus groups and market research aren't enough to keep companies flourishing. Procter & Gamble is looking outside the company, tapping the Internet to find innovators, while Best Buy is reaching out to Silicon Valley start-ups and teaming up with entrepreneurs to bring new products to market.

The company created two entirely new brands in a matter of weeks. Aided by design firm IDEO Inc., Jackson Enterprises brought together people from all parts of the business for a weeklong off-site brainstorming session, a first for the company, that shook up managers. In December 2004, the whole group decamped for Palo Alto, a two-hour drive from the company's headquarters in wine country, for a series of mind-expanding exercises. IDEO did all sorts of things to bring fresh points of view into the discussions, including inviting Stanford students with no background in wine to sit in. One of the key lessons for Lee was rapid prototyping, quickly patching together rough models of wine concepts so that the group could see how they looked.

The team emerged from the marathon with 10 crazy ideas, then settled on two of the less crazy ones. One, named by corporate attorney Tiffanie Di Liberty, was Wine Block, the first wine-in-a-box ever for Jackson. These are elegant 1.5-liter cubes modeled on perfume packaging. The second was Dog House. These bottles have twist-off tops and a drawing of a dopey dog on the label. The price is $6.99, half that of a typical Kendall-Jackson bottle. Another departure: to get the wine ready for delivery in April 2005, they used a mobile bottling plant installed in the back of a semi in the parking lot.

The results have a hearty bouquet. Jackson expected to sell about 10,000 cases of each. Instead, both broke the 100,000-case barrier. The company has an even bolder new venture in the works, which is hush-hush for now.

POWER PLAY

It's common for companies to fall back on old habits and old thinking. To avoid that trap, brainstorm off-site and/or with outsiders. When Jackson Enterprises was facing a glut of wine, it used that method to come up with two successful new concepts for selling wine.

HAND OFF TASKS TO SPECIALISTS

Outsourcing companies don't just do things more cheaply anymore; they can do them better and faster. Take the cell phone business. What's in vogue changes as rapidly as clothing fashions, so companies must introduce a steady stream of new designs. The problem is, it typically takes 12 to 18 months to develop a phone from scratch. That's why cell phone companies, both leaders and also-rans, are tapping outfits such as Cellon Inc. in San Jose, California, to design some or all of their models.

Cellon doesn't wait for customers to call before it starts engineering. It has a half-dozen basic designs that it can quickly customize for a particular client. These designs include the chips and circuitry for various networks and combinations of features. Cellon, with operations in China, works with nearby manufacturers to prepare its designs for production. It takes just five months to go from design to market. That's crucial. The life span of a cell phone model is now about nine months. If it takes 18 months to design a product, it's obsolete before it hits the market. In five years, 30 million phones designed by Cellon have been sold by the likes of Haier, Royal Philips Electronics, UTStarcom, and some leading brands it is not allowed to name.

POWER PLAY

Thriving companies often repeat their successes by using the same technology or business model in new markets. Virgin launched a mobile service in Britain, and then used the same template in three other countries.

ONCE YOU HAVE IT RIGHT, REPEAT

Virgin took just six months to launch its first mobile phone service in Britain in 1999. That was mainly because the company arranged with a cell phone service provider to use an existing network rather than take the time and money required to build its own. Since then, Virgin has begun phone service in three countries using the same model, and it expects to launch in three more this year. By using the wireless networks of other companies, Virgin can concentrate on the marketing and customer service that it does best. "It's a template. We'll roll out in a new country every four to five months. It's fast and lean," says Will Whitehorn, Virgin's development director.

Fast and lean has a nice ring to it, but it's not a claim that many companies can make. While some organizations have speeded up their innovation and formation of new businesses, they're the exceptions. Most are still bogged down in bureaucracy and old modes of doing things. That's a recipe for trouble. "There are two kinds of businesses: the quick and the

POWER PLAY

One way to speed up the product-development process is to build alliances or outsource tasks to specialists. XM and Samsung teamed up to produce a co-branded portable satellite radio in just nine months. Cell phone designer Cellon customizes designs for its clients, enabling them to produce phones in just five months.

dead," warns analyst Bruce Richardson of tech industry consultancy AMR Research Inc. That's probably an overstatement. But in an era in which once-mighty dinosaurs are struggling to survive, the alternative to fast and lean may soon be . . . gone.

NEW DIRECTIONS

Various measures are being taken to instill new life into businesses:

- Companies have learned to cut back on the layers of decision makers that can kill new ideas or slow down the process.
- Successful ideas are maximized by reusing them in different markets.
- At large companies, small teams with "fences" around them are free to promulgate new ideas without getting tangled in red tape.
- The Internet is increasingly being used to find promising innovations outside the company.
- Status quo thinking inside the company is avoided by holding brainstorming sessions out of the office.

This cover story by Steve Hamm, with Ian Rowley appeared in the March 27, 2006 issue.

FIVE COMMON MISTAKES
IN INNOVATION

Every company knows how to become more innovative,
but few are willing to make the cultural changes necessary
to get results.

There's a growing consensus around what it takes to be
truly innovative. Launch some great new products and services.
Encourage your people to take risks. Get started on the long,
hard work of creating metrics and processes that help employees
engage with new ideas. That's what the world's most innovative
companies are doing. But just because you know how to do
something doesn't mean that you will do it.

We all know what kind of exercise and diet it takes to
develop rock-hard, six-pack abs. While many of us would like
to look lean and muscular, a regimen of constant crunches and
low-calorie meals is hard to maintain over the course of years.
Innovation works the same way. Everybody knows how
to become more innovative, but they are rarely willing to
undertake the kinds of cultural changes that are necessary
to yield significant results. Without more actionable advice,
too many companies proceed to make the same mistakes
when trying to spark innovation.

OVERRELIANCE ON PILOT INITIATIVES

"We'll be more innovative if we do more brainstorming sessions."

In an attempt to take action quickly, some companies
initiate projects that focus on a single product idea or a
promising near-term opportunity. Alternatively, they latch on
to a single technique, such as ethnographies or brainstorming.
Yet for most companies, the scale of the impact required is too
massive to depend on a single approach.

Recognizing this, successful companies such as Procter &
Gamble are taking a portfolio approach to innovation, working

with multiple consultants and using multiple methods so that the process of innovation becomes a series of multiple experiments. They then come away with a better understanding of not only which methods and partners work, but which ones work best with their existing organizational culture.

UNHEALTHY FASCINATION WITH UNIQUE CHARISMATIC EXAMPLES

"Steve Jobs is so cool: We need to be more like him."

It's difficult to have a discussion on innovation without invoking the names of charismatic visionaries such as Steve Jobs or Richard Branson. Apple and Virgin, along with Nike, Starbucks, and other media darlings, certainly make for great storytelling. Unfortunately, they also serve as lousy models for the rest of us.

Enticing as they are, such cases too often depend on a kind of business leader who is, for better or worse, nonexistent in most companies. If you work for Steve Jobs, innovation seems like second nature. If you don't, the only useful lesson seems to be to quit your job and go work for Apple.

MISAPPLICATION OF OTHER COMPANIES' APPROACHES

"P&G is using a 'connect and develop' strategy, so we should, too."

It can be more enlightening, but equally dangerous, to emulate the approaches of other companies. P&G has recently received much attention for its "connect and develop" strategy, whereby the company reaches out to promising entrepreneurs, scientists, and consumers in the hopes of mainstreaming the ideas that they present. IBM has received similar praise for its experiments with "open innovation." Such strategies are far more useful than those that rely on charismatic individuals.

At the same time, these approaches work because they're tailored to the conditions of the companies in question. "Connect and develop" is a wonderful strategy for P&G because of who it is, the categories it plays in, and the company's structural systems and DNA. Just because something is good for P&G doesn't mean that it will be good for the rest of us. The mechanical application of inappropriate methods has led to the failure of more than one innovation program.

DESCENT INTO A CYCLE OF SELF-RECRIMINATION
"Our people just aren't creative enough."

Looking to external sources of inspiration can sometimes have further unintended consequences if the firm decides that it can never measure up to the level of external case studies. It's not unusual for innovation planning teams to benchmark other companies, only to come away feeling that their own problems are insurmountable. As it turns out, they may be looking in the wrong place.

Companies such as 3M are instead returning to what has made them great in the past. It's a generalized form of what organizational-change experts call appreciative inquiry: search inside yourself for moments of greatness, determine which activities spurred these moments of greatness, and then figure out how to do more of that. Virtually no companies in the Fortune 500 got where they are by accident. Savvy leaders capitalize on their organizations' strengths and capabilities to create sustainable approaches to growth that are appropriate to their inherent cultures.

RESIGNATION TO SUPERFICIAL CHANGES
"Let's just paint the walls purple."

Perhaps most depressing of all are the companies that turn away from significant structural improvement in favor of cosmetic changes. After benchmarking several Silicon Valley companies, one firm noticed that many of the companies it admired had yellow and purple walls. The team members went back and painted the walls of their offices yellow and purple, thinking that this might actually make them more innovative. While color can influence behavior, and there's something important to be said about the effect of environment on creativity, such initiatives alone usually aren't enough to actually change the DNA of the organization.

CHANGING THE GAME

A few years into the business fad of innovation, the conversation around the space is changing. Some companies, such as General Electric, played around with quick hits, harvested the low-hanging fruit in front of them, and moved on to the next thing. Other companies, such as Ford, have draped themselves in innovation terminology, only to keep on doing business the way they always have.

The companies that are realizing the biggest bang for their innovation buck, however, aren't on the front page anymore. While out of the public eye, companies such as Hewlett-Packard have been digging deep and doing the long, hard work of transforming into innovation leaders for the long term. They can see that the script for innovation isn't a mystery. It just takes a long time and a lot of change to pull off. That's why right now we're discovering just who has the game and who just wants to claim the title of innovation to look good.

This article by Dev Patnaik appeared on October 19, 2007.

MAKING ONLINE PAY

There's interesting news from Europe about online content and underlying business models along the free-to-paying continuum. Here are three of them.

Daniel Schneidermann is launching an online TV show that will be the first in the world to be supported by its subscribers— rather than by advertising only.

Schneidermann is probably a nobody to most people outside of France, but in his own country he is a famous cultural critic who used to host a well-regarded media analysis TV show, *Arrêt sur Images*, which translates as *Freeze-Frame*. His role as the watchdog's watchdog has gained him a broad following, as well as many enemies in newsrooms. Last June, under the pretext of implementing an overhaul to its program roster, France5 (a public channel) dropped the show. Within a month, 185,000 fans signed a protest petition.

More than 15,000 of those people (so far) have also put their money where their pens were and promised to pay €30 ($42) per year to subscribe to his new online show, *@rretsurimages*, which will start on January 7, 2008. The subscription campaign continues for what is likely to be a weekly show complemented by daily news, blogs, and a free general news section.

Schneidermann is not an easy character; he borders on the cantankerous, but that comes with the job. And he does his job well, which is, of course, the core of his appeal: high-quality unique content. On the site arretsurimages.net, which currently is still little more than a blog, he recently has been dissecting the contortions of the French press as it tries not to pay too much attention to a letter photographed from a distance in the hands of President Nicolas Sarkozy. The letter looked like a love note, but that's not Schneidermann's subject. His focus is on how the media treated that picture—including why one paper published it only after having photoshopped out the text from the paper held by Sarkozy.

FREE FOR A WHILE

The London *Financial Times* is not ready to let go of the idea of making people pay for its online news and analysis. But it seems to have learned a lesson from the recent decision by the *New York Times* to terminate its TimesSelect premium content section.

The British business newspaper is trying to find a way to get subscriber money, while at the same time making sure that its content maintains the broadest possible impact. Starting in mid-October, the *FT* will introduce an innovative charging scheme: articles and data will be free to users up to a total of 30 views a month. They will then be asked to subscribe for access to more material. If that doesn't sound particularly avant-garde, consider the motivation: the change would allow bloggers and news aggregators to link to material that was previously available only to subscribers.

Despite the $10 million or so that TimesSelect was bringing in, the *New York Times* had discovered a couple of major hidden costs of putting its best columnists behind a paying wall: doing so reduced their chances of being found by search engines and online news aggregators (Netheads call that GoogleJuice) and kept them out of important portions of the public conversations, thus reducing their influence—and the influence of the newspaper. The *FT* is trying not to repeat the mistake.

STEAL THIS CD

The music event of this season will be the release of rock band Radiohead's new album, *In Rainbows*. That's partly because of the music, from one of the world's most innovative bands, but also because of the way the band is releasing it: it's giving it away.

In Rainbows will be available only via the band's Web site (inrainbows.com). Consumers place the digital files into their "shopping basket," and when they get to the payment page, there is a question mark listed as the price, and they're told, "It's up to you"—you name your own price, and it's totally acceptable for that price to be zero. (You can already preorder. Downloads will be activated on October 10.)

On the site, you can also buy the physical version of *In Rainbows*: a box containing the new album on CD; the new album on two long-playing vinyl records; a second CD with more new songs, photographs, and artwork; an artwork booklet; and a booklet of lyrics. Plus, the download is thrown in as a freebie. The artwork is by Stanley Donwood, Radiohead's longtime collaborator. The boxes are priced at £40 ($85), including postage, and they will be shipped around December 3.

EXPERIMENTAL BUSINESS MODEL

Radiohead is going off-label, letting people download their music for as much or as little as they want (without copyright protection) and then offering, for a high price, a sophisticated and unexpected (the vinyl) multi-item package that borders on being a collector's item. The off-label part is not a real surprise, since the band's contract with EMI expired after its last record in 2003. Many thought that Radiohead's next album might be released through iTunes or other established online music stores. That the band would skip even that step and go solo, directly to fans—that's the surprise.

The business model here is a matter of pure experimentation, but it challenges most aspects of the current music industry model. By giving away digital music, the group is turning it into a loss leader and hoping that it will boost the sales of the boxed set and of concert tickets (the concert business, by the way, is booming).

CUTTING OUT THE MIDDLEMAN

Radiohead seems to be adhering to a statement given to *Time* magazine by lead singer Thom Yorke a few years back: "I like the people at our record company, but the time is at hand when you have to ask why anyone needs one."

This approach is likely to work well for stars with name recognition and huge fan bases. A few months ago, the singer Prince gave away his last album as an insert in a tabloid newspaper in Britain. The music industry and store owners protested, but the move certainly helped him sell out all of his 21 London concert dates.

But it may take longer for the music industry to work out the ramifications of these innovative approaches to music distribution—both as a whole and for younger, upcoming artists. For now, go online, name your price, and enjoy the music.

This article by Bruno Giussani appeared on October 8, 2007.

HP'S CULTURAL REVOLUTION

At Hewlett-Packard's Page Mill Road complex in Palo Alto, California, in the basement beneath the meticulously preserved offices of founders William Hewlett and David Packard, is a cavernous room that has the feel of a chaotic startup. Tables and chairs are strewn about and a giant, makeshift screen takes up an entire wall, even wrapping around a corner. HP projectors made for corporate presentations are clustered together to cast huge video-game images on the wall. The life-size scenes are so crisp and detailed that you almost feel as if you could walk onto a Madden NFL game or Halo 3 battle.

This game room is the kind of place where you would expect to find young programmers hanging out, jazzed on Mountain Dew and revving up ideas for a new 3-D Web or the next generation of social media. It's a different business culture from the one you'll find in the gray cubicles, where most engineers work, in the rest of the building. The area's playful environment is critical to HP's future. The space—and its projection system, itself a prototype—is one result of the Innovation Program Office, launched in 2006 to help the info tech giant buy hip, nimble startups for its huge Personal Systems Group, which makes PCs, mobile devices, and workstations. The hope is to inject big doses of small companies' creative juices directly into the HP culture.

HP has learned some key lessons on the acquisition trail over the past two years: how to develop cool, high-margin products that appeal to new consumer groups such as video-game fanatics; how to use social media to conduct Web-based consumer research; and, perhaps most important, how to inspire engineers in HP Laboratories to turn concepts into products faster.

HP's culture has been in turmoil in recent years. The HP Way, the company's management code, was once Silicon Valley's innovation model. Top executives mingled with lower-level employees to discover fresh ideas. For decades, the company's engineer-led approach generated a flow of popular, affordable, and utilitarian products until it became synonymous with complacency and high costs. Carleton "Carly" S. Fiorina came in as chief executive in 1999 and tried to blow apart that culture. Her marketing-focused strategy generated strong sales but demoralized employees. Mark V. Hurd, who succeeded her in 2005, has been working to restore tradition and reinvigorate the company's 30,000 engineers.

Trouble is, restoring the HP Way may no longer be enough. The old strategy was for engineers to create technologies and products and then expect customers to buy them. Yet over the past five years the company's businesses—computers, printers and imaging machines, storage devices and servers, and info tech service—as well as those of Dell, Cisco, and Yahoo!—have shifted their focus from developing cool technologies to making products customers want. "We were missing the DNA of an organization that had its finger on customer desires," says Phil McKinney, a chief technology officer of the Personal Systems Group and head of the innovation office.

HP is trying to market personal computers today as being friendly, not just fast and powerful. Its slogan: "The computer is personal again." It's not just selling fast printers, but pitching terrific printing experiences. But shifting away from a tech focus to a consumer orientation is proving hard for a 156,000-person company that includes a small army of engineers convinced they are right.

Enter Voodoo PC. The gaming room at HP was the brainchild of Voodoo's Rahul Sood, co-founder of the 30-person startup based in Calgary, Canada, a cult brand among gamers. Now 35, Sood is chief technology officer of HP's new global gaming business unit.

The tech giant snapped up Voodoo because it's a fan-based, gamer-driven company with a devoted following for its luxe offerings, from lipstick-red PCs to customized $50,000 PCs tricked out with jewels and leather. The machines have cut-out panels that reveal their complex innards—the typical Voodoo units are about as far as possible from the commoditized, no- nonsense gray boxes that HP sells. Sood himself is a fierce gamer, and he began the outfit with his brother to make better machines for himself and his friends. Gamers, not techies, run the business. At Voodoo, "we took the ultimate wish list from customers and rolled it into the product line," says Sood, who has gelled, spiky hair and rectangular hipster glasses. He's now helping to bring that customer-centric DNA to the 600 engineers and researchers who inhabit the huge company's research labs.

"When I first walked into HP Labs, I thought, 'Everyone is smarter than me. They know more about the tech and fundamentals of research.' But I brought a completely different perspective. They don't know what gamers want or need. . . . No one [at HP] had ever figured this out."

So how is Voodoo, the innovation unit's initial project, changing its new parent? The first fruit of the acquisition, the HP Blackbird 002 personal computer, was available for preorders online in September and hit stores this month. The PC was originally designed by an outside shop, but HP scrapped that plan and redesigned the machine with Voodoo after the deal. It has distinctively Voodoo—and un-HP— touches such as a customizable black metal panel with elegant geometric designs and a liquid cooling system that replaces the distracting hum of fans. It's so user-friendly that consumers who want to customize it themselves can do so without using tools. It takes 10 seconds to replace or upgrade a hard drive on Blackbird—a job that typically requires 30 minutes. Although it's a premium PC (priced at $2,500 to $5,000) aimed primarily at hard-core gamers, the high-margin machine was purchased by film editors, animators, medical imaging specialists, an energy trader, a plastic surgeon, and even Navy SEALs, according to the company. It's a powerful, fast computer with room for five hard drives to accommodate rich graphics.

Curious HP engineers, frustrated at not being able to translate their ideas into products quickly, have been making pilgrimages to the gaming room. Chat up researchers at HP Labs, and the tension between engineers and the suits is clear.

"There's an overabundance of ideas in our labs, but there's a gap between labs and product development," says Patrick Goddi, a senior researcher. Before the innovation office was created, he says, "It was hard to get a sense of oomph."

Goddi and various other researchers who are avid gamers visit the room in their spare time. After hearing about the speed (just three months) in which Sood pushed the projector system from a mere idea toward a prototype shown at trade shows, Goddi says he felt a rush of energy. With new confidence, he pursued a potential product aimed at gamers based on his current project, a video-messaging service called Conversa, a cross between YouTube and e-mail. "Rahul fired us up to build something, and to bring fun to work," he says. Goddi was inspired, he says, to develop Conversa as a social-networking tool for online games.

Startups are even providing HP with a new customer-based system that accelerates product development in other divisions. Snapfish, an online photo-sharing service acquired by HP in 2005 with more than 42 million members now, inspired an experiment called Snapfish Labs that begins this month. Targeted members of Snapfish vote on proposals coming out of HP Labs and provide instant feedback. One upcoming idea: a service that allows people at conferences to upload, manipulate, and archive photos of meeting materials, including the writing on whiteboards, and share it with people not attending. (The jury is still out—the votes haven't been tallied yet.) Snapfish Labs has boosted the rate of customer-focused innovation because consumers can weigh in early on potential HP products. "We're bringing raw projects to the market more quickly," says Patrick Scaglia, who oversees the strategy of the corporation's Imaging & Printing Group. "Before, this was a challenge," he says. "We had a long investment cycle. We'd go with one idea a year. Sometimes it would take 10 years to get a good idea [to market]."

The process itself of buying startups is teaching HP some hard lessons. Take Tabblo, acquired in 2007. It's an online printing service that allows members of social media sites to format content such as pictures so they look better when printed. Users can, for example, create their own slick postcards. In October, Tabblo and HP announced a partnership with Flickr, the popular photo-sharing and social-networking site acquired by Yahoo. But in putting the deal together, cultures clashed. The HP suits "expected that everything we were going to do was going to be defined by business development, legal, and finance executives. They'd expected to talk about the [partnership] contract for a few months," says Tabblo founder Antonio Rodriguez. "But we were used to time scales of days, not weeks or months." Tabblo surprised the suits by signing the contract and releasing the Flickr service in only six weeks—vs. an expected three to four months—thanks to a casual relationship between Flickr and Tabblo execs that didn't involve lengthy bureaucratic talks. It was a wake-up call for HP. "What has been dramatic in the last year since we acquired Tabblo is that we suddenly have injected inside HP a Web culture we never had before," says Scaglia.

OLD SCHOOL RESISTANCE?

Throughout Silicon Valley, acquisitions-as-usual are changing, too. In the past, big established companies usually bought agile startups mostly for new technologies and products. One popular model has been to buy companies and keep them independent to maintain their creativity much like Google and YouTube or News Corp. and MySpace. Or Dell and Alienware, Voodoo's rival in the hard-core gamer PC market.

When large corporations do try to change the ways they encourage creativity, they don't typically go out and buy new companies. Sure, Xerox, Boeing, and IBM sometimes create "skunkworks" teams to help speed cutting-edge technologies. But these groups usually work on projects independent of corporate reporting policies and structures. Other companies build venture-capital units, like Intel Capital, which vet and fund the development of internal as well as external projects. But these incubated businesses remain isolated from the larger corporation.

What HP, Yahoo!, Cisco, and others are doing now is different. Their new strategy is innovation via absorption—and that's very hard to do. "It's difficult to infuse the acquirer's culture with the target's culture," says Saikat Chaudhuri, a Wharton School assistant professor of management who's followed the tactic for a decade. Even HP's McKinney admits: "Companies have to realize this isn't a quick fix. It isn't business process re-engineering. This is a fundamental shift in the culture of an organization."

HP has embraced many kinds of innovation in recent years. The acquisition of Compaq, for example, changed the nature of its business. Hurd's move to raise efficiency and cut costs changed its many processes. Now, it's inciting a cultural change. And the company that began as the prototypical story of two guys experimenting in a garage is trying to see the world through the fresh eyes of a startup. Again.

This November 15, 2007 article by Reena Jana showcases how HP has picked up the pace of innovation by betting on startups and injecting their DNA into its operations.

SOURCES

Chapter 1: Steve Hamm, with Louise Lee and Spencer E. Ante, "Kodak's Moment of Truth," February 2007; http://www.businessweek.com/magazine/content/07_08/b4022048.htm?chan=search.

Chapter 2: Michelle Conlin, "No Schedules, No Meetings, No Joke at Best Buy," December 2006; http://www.businessweek.com/magazine/content/06_50/b4013001.htm?chan=search.

Chapter 3: Jay Greene with Peter Burrows, "The Soul of a New Microsoft," December 2006; http://www.businessweek.com/magazine/content/06_49/b4012001.htm?chan=search.

Chapter 4: Mara Der Hovanesian with Emily Thornton, Stanley Reed, and Joseph Weber, "JPMorgan's Grand Design," March 28, 2005; http://www.businessweek.com/magazine/content/05_13/b3926103_mz020.htm.

Chapter 5: Gail Edmondson, "BMW's Dream Factory," 2006; http://www.businessweek.com/magazine/content/06_42/b4005072.htm.

Chapter 6: Carol Matlack, Diane Brady, Robert Berner, Rachel Tiplady, and Hiroko Tashiro, "The Vuitton Money Machine," 2004; http://www.businessweek.com/magazine/content/04_12/b3875002.htm.

Chapter 7: Andy Reinhardt, "A Sea Change in Software at SAP," 2005; http://www.businessweek.com/magazine/content/05_28/b3942075_mz054.htm

Chapter 8: Michael Arndt, "Why Kraft Is on a Crash Diet," 2004; http://www.businessweek.com/magazine/content/04_48/b3910058_mz011.htm.

Chapter 9:   Tom Lowry, "Repositioning Any Brand with Pop Culture," 2007; http://www.businessweek.com/magazine/content/07_13/b4027062.htm?chan=search.

TRENDS: Steve Hamm, with Ian Rowley, "Speed Demons," 2006; http://www.businessweek.com/magazine/content/06_13/b3977001.htm?chan=search.

VIEWPOINT: Dev Patnaik, "Five Common Mistakes in Innovation," October 19, 2007; http://www.businessweek.com/innovate/content/oct2007/id20071019_786269.htm

VIEWPOINT: Bruno Giussani, "Making Online Pay," October 8, 2007;http://www.businessweek.com/innovate/content/oct2007/id2007108_518727.htm

VIEWPOINT: Reena Jana, "HP's Cultural Revolution," November 15, 2007;http://www.businessweek.com/innovate/content/nov2007/id20071114_289027_page_3.htm

CONTRIBUTORS

SPENCER E. ANTE is the computer department editor for *BusinessWeek*. He is responsible for covering computer hardware, software, chips and services, with a focus on the tech industry's biggest company, IBM. Previously, Mr. Ante was Internet department editor.

Mr. Ante has been writing about technology and business for the last eight years. Before joining *BusinessWeek* in February 2000, he was a staff reporter covering the Internet for *TheStreet.com*. Prior to that, he was a contributing writer at *Wired News,* a columnist for *Business 2.0,* and a producer for the Netscape NetCenter.

A New York and New Jersey native, Mr. Ante received a bachelor's degree from the Kelley School of Business at Indiana University and a master's degree in journalism from the University of California at Berkeley.

MICHAEL ARNDT was named editor of *BusinessWeek*'s new monthly, BW Chicago, in August, after 7 years in the magazine's Chicago bureau as a senior correspondent. While at *BusinessWeek*, he has covered virtually every business beat, from pharmaceuticals and health care to manufacturing, from airlines to retail and fast food. He has also edited various sections of the magazine.

Before joining *BusinessWeek* at the start of 2000, Mr. Arndt was a business editor at the *Chicago Tribune* for five years, overseeing a staff of up to two dozen reporters and was directly responsible for the paper's Sunday business section. He was chief economics correspondent for the *Tribune* in its Washington, DC, bureau from 1990 to 1995. He became a business reporter in 1987, after seven years as a metro reporter in the city and suburbs. During his career at the *Tribune*, Mr. Arndt reported from Russia, Mexico, Canada and Japan. His first job in Chicago was at the now defunct City News bureau.

ROBERT BERNER is a correspondent in *BusinessWeek*'s Chicago bureau, responsible for coverage of retailing.

Prior to joining *BusinessWeek*, Mr. Berner wrote for the *Wall Street Journal,* covering retailers, drugstores, grocers and food companies. In 1985, he began his journalism career as a reporter for the *Bennington Banner* in Vermont. After leaving the *Banner*, Mr. Berner became a business reporter for the *Patriot Ledger*. Mr. Berner is a graduate of Oberlin College

PETER BURROWS is a senior writer at *BusinessWeek*, a position he assumed in early 2007. He has been a member of the magazine's Silicon Valley bureau since 1995, covering various segments of high tech, including computers, networking and digital media. From 1993 to 1995, he was a correspondent in the Dallas bureau, covering tech and the energy sector.

MICHELLE CONLIN is the editor of the Working Life Department at *BusinessWeek*. She co-edited *BusinessWeek*'s award-winning cover story on the Catholic Church. Prior to *BusinessWeek*, Ms. Conlin was a staff writer for *Forbes*. Previously, she was a correspondent for the *Philadelphia Inquirer*. Ms. Conlin is a graduate of the Columbia University Graduate School of Journalism, where she was the recipient of the Richard T. Baker prize for best print reporting.

GAIL EDMONDSON covered European business as a senior correspondent in *BusinessWeek*'s Frankfurt bureau. Previously, she held the position of Rome bureau chief, a position she assumed in October 1999.

In 1994, Ms. Edmondson was appointed to the position of European technology correspondent based in Paris, where she was responsible for covering technology trends and companies throughout Europe. Ms. Edmondson became the Paris bureau chief three years later. Ms. Edmondson holds a bachelor's degree in American studies from Cornell University and a master's in communications from Stanford. She is the winner of a fellowship offered by Bosch, the West German maker of auto equipment, which gives 15 "future leaders of America" an opportunity to gain an informed understanding of German culture, society, and business. She also received an Amos Tuck School of Business Journalism award for a series on the economic indicators.

BRUNO GIUSSANI is a Swiss writer, tech entrepreneur, conference host, and the author of "Roam: Making Sense of the Wireless Internet." He blogs at http://www.LunchOverIP.com.

JAY GREENE joined *BusinessWeek* in January 2000. He started as a member of the San Mateo, California, bureau, based in Seattle. A year later, he opened the two-correspondent Seattle office and became bureau chief. In addition to overseeing the bureau, he is responsible for technology coverage in the Pacific Northwest.

Mr. Greene has been a reporter for a wide range of publications. Prior to joining *BusinessWeek*, he was the Microsoft reporter for the *Seattle Times*. He also worked as a business reporter for the *Orange County Register* in Santa Ana, California, where he covered healthcare. Before that, he was a film and finance reporter for *Variety* in Los Angeles, California, covering the entertainment industry. He was also a business reporter *for* the *Plain Dealer in Cleveland, Ohio,* the *Daily News in Los Angeles, California,* and the *Press Enterprise* in Riverside, California.

STEVE HAMM is a senior writer at *BusinessWeek* attached to the information technology team. He writes about technology, globalization, innovation, and leadership. He also writes a blog for BusinessWeek Online, Bangalore Tigers, about the offshoring of work.

He has worked for *BusinessWeek* for 10 years, starting in Silicon Valley and then moving to New York in 1999. His book, *Bangalore Tigers,* about the rise of the Indian tech industry, was published by McGraw-Hill Professional Books in 2006.

MARA DER HOVANESIAN is the finance and banking department editor at *BusinessWeek*.

Before joining *BusinessWeek* in May 2000, she covered the mutual fund and personal finance industries for Dow Jones & Co. and Knight Ridder newspapers. Her work has appeared in the *Wall Street Journal* and other major metropolitan newspapers nationwide.

Ms. Der Hovanesian received her master's degree in economics from California State University in San Francisco in 1990. She won a first place award from the Associated Press for Business Writing in 1996 and a Scholarship to the Institute for Political Journalism at Georgetown University in 1986.

REENA JANA is the Innovation Department editor for *BusinessWeek*. Prior to this position, she was a staff writer at BusinessWeek.com, covering innovation and design. Previously, Jana was a free-lance writer for national publications (including the *New York Times* and *Wired*) specializing in the intersection of emerging technologies and culture. She is co-author of the book *New Media Art* (Taschen, 2006) and a former National Arts Journalism Program Fellow at Columbia Journalism School. Jana received a bachelor's degree from Barnard College and a master's in South Asian studies from Columbia .

LOUISE LEE is a correspondent in the *BusinessWeek* San Mateo, California, bureau. She is responsible for covering nontechnology companies in the Bay area. Prior to *BusinessWeek*, Lee wrote for the *Asian Wall Street Journal*, where she spearheaded a bimonthly column devoted to Asian marketing topics. She also spent four years in the *Journal's* Dallas bureau, covering such major retailers as Wal-Mart Stores and J.C. Penney. Before the *Journal*, she worked as a business reporter at the *Oakland Tribune* and the *Peninsula Times Tribune* in Palo Alto, California. Lee has degrees from both Princeton University and Stanford University.

TOM LOWRY is a senior writer for *BusinessWeek*, responsible for the magazine's media and entertainment coverage. Prior to this position, Mr. Lowry was media editor for the magazine. He has penned and/or edited six cover stories since 2004, including "Can MTV Stay Cool?," a profile of CEO Judy McGrath and her efforts to remake her company for a digital world; "ESPN, The Empire," an analysis of how the hottest brand in sports plans to stay on top of rivals; and "Rupert's World," one of the first articles to add up all the Aussie mogul's vast and growing powers. Another cover "MegaMerger" dealt with Comcast's hostile bid for Disney. He also wrote "Yao!," a sports biz story on the Chinese basketball phenom.

Other cover story subjects have included the Vanishing Mass Market, Dick Parsons, Comcast, the NFL, and Bloomberg LP.

Lowry is an alum of the University of Delaware, and was a Knight-Bagehot Fellow in Business and Economics Journalism at the Columbia Graduate School of Journalism. A newspaper veteran, he also did stints at the New York *Daily News* and *USA Today*, among others, before coming to *BusinessWeek* in 1999.

CAROL MATLACK has been Paris bureau chief for *BusinessWeek* since 2005. She was a correspondent in the Paris bureau for five years before that, covering business, economic, and political news. She joined *BusinessWeek* in 1996 as a special correspondent in the Moscow bureau. Prior to that, she was managing editor of *National Journal* magazine in Washington, DC. Earlier, she was a reporter for the *Arkansas Gazette* newspaper. She is a graduate of Oberlin College.

DEV PATNAIK is the managing associate of Jump Associates. Jump helps companies build new businesses, define new products and services, and create cultures of innovation.

STANLEY REED has been London bureau chief of *BusinessWeek* since August 1996. He took on the additional role of Middle East correspondent in 1999. Prior to London, he held a series of editing positions at *BusinessWeek* in New York. He lived in Cairo from 1976–1980 and has written for the *New York Times*,

Foreign Affairs, and *Foreign Policy*. He is a graduate of Yale University and Columbia Business School. He was a Knight-Bagehot Fellow at Columbia University Journalism School in 1987–1988. He was president of the Association of American Correspondents in London for 1998 and remains a member of its executive board.

ANDY REINHARDT is a correspondent in *BusinessWeek*'s Paris bureau. He is responsible for covering technology in Europe. In addition, he is Europe channel editor for BusinessWeek.com. In 1996, Reinhardt joined *BusinessWeek* as a Silicon Valley correspondent. In 1999, he was named Silicon Valley deputy bureau chief. Previously, Reinhardt was an executive editor for *PC World*. Prior to that, he was the West Coast bureau chief of *Byte*. He is a graduate of Harvard College and Columbia University Graduate School of Journalism.

IAN ROWLEY is a correspondent based in *BusinessWeek*'s Tokyo bureau, covering a range of beats, including autos, finance, and retail. Before moving to Japan in 2003, Rowley spent several years in London as a magazine writer, specializing in banking and finance. He holds a master's degree from the London School of Economics.

HIROKO TASHIRO is a correspondent for *BusinessWeek* based in Tokyo.

EMILY THORNTON is an associate editor for *BusinessWeek*. Previously, she was the investment banking editor and a Tokyo correspondent. Before *BusinessWeek*, she was a correspondent for the *Far Eastern Economic Review* based in Hong Kong. Prior to that, she was a Tokyo correspondent for *Fortune*. She won a Detroit Press Foundation award. Thornton is a graduate of Princeton University. She is also a 2000 executive MBA graduate from Temple University.

RACHEL TIPLADY worked in *BusinessWeek*'s London bureau.

JOSEPH WEBER is chief of correspondents for *BusinessWeek*, based in Chicago. Previously, he was Chicago bureau manager. Weber joined *BusinessWeek* in June 1987 as a correspondent in Dallas. He was Philadelphia bureau manager from January 1988 until August, 1997. He then managed Canadian coverage from Toronto until December 1999. Among his many awards are an Excellence in Financial Journalism award from the New York State Society of CPAs, two Peter Lisagor awards from the Headline Club of Chicago, and a Distinguished Editorial Achievement award from McGraw-Hill. Weber is a graduate of Rutgers University and Columbia University Graduate School of Journalism.